AKURIAN METAPHYSICAL HANDBOOK
VOLUME I

To Wit: "**No Bill of Attainder or ex post facto Law shall be passed.**"; noting that much of these Doctrines of True Righteousness contained herein were enscribed and otherwise recorded prior to the deliberate desecrations of said Holy Document, The Constitution of the United States of America, making such content illegal, were enacted into law; specifically the language recorded therein, which in some instances is not appropriate for the immature and minor children and we do advise parental/guardian guidance with respect thereto.

We await the One World Government socialist's attacks and abominations ...

The Akurians.

Below are the **O**ne **W**orld **G**overnment
Legislated Enslavement numbers,
and
One **W**orld **G**overnment Seal of Damnation
as *required* by law to sell this book.
ISBN-13: 978-0615458748
ISBN-10: 0615458742

www.TheAkurians.com
The Akurians
Post Office Box 3456
Albuquerque NM 87190 USA
Tel: 505-796-4651

Printed under authority of The Akurians
and Authorized by
The Anointed of God PATHFINDERS of Elijah, Inc.

Blanket permission to quote in-part granted
if accompanied by the statement:
(© The Akurians, used by permission.)

First Printing, 2011

THE BRIEFINGS PRIOR TO AND
AUDIENCE BEFORE THE MOST HIGH

DEDICATION

For Support and Assistance
Above and Beyond the Call of Duty:

Command Marshal General D. Chylon Budagher, P.K.,
Grand Council of Gnostics, 2010-2015

Command Marshal General Peter K. Shams-Avari, P.K.,
Grand Council of Gnostics, 2010-2015

Supreme General David B. Schipul, P.K.
South East US Corps Command

Staff General Rosalind R. Clark, P.K.,
Grand Council of Gnostics, 2010-2015

Brigadier General Diane D. Meinke, P.K.,
Grand Council of Gnostics, 2010-2015

Brigadier General Kathryn Anne Malone, P.K.,
Grand Council of Gnostics, 2010-2015

Brigadier General Patrique Murphy-Siler, P.K.,
Grand Council of Gnostics, 2010-2015

Brigadier General Erich M. Headrick, III, P.K.,
Grand Council of Gnostics, 2010-2015

Major Gareld D. Riggs, P.K.,
Senior Officer, State of Arizona

Major Janita Jean Kilpatrick, P.K.,
Senior Officer, State of New York

AKURIAN METAPHYSICIAN'S HANDBOOK
Volume I

By The Akurians.
Copyright 2011, The Akurians.
All Rights Reserved.
International Copyright Secured.

The Most High Lord God of All Creation, The Most High Supreme Lord of Spirits, the God of Ish (*Adam*) and Isha (*Eve*), the God of Enoch, the God of Noe (*Noah*), the God of Shem, the God of Melchizedek, the God of Audreah, the God of Abraham, the God of Ishmael (*Arabia*), the God of Isaac, and the God of Jacob (*Israel*) *will personally communicate with YOU, the individual!*

Just be prepared to understand *YOU* have been lied to all your life, *about everything!* And be prepared to possess the *True Spiritual Knowledge YOU* have been deliberately deprived of:

When *The Most High, Himself, Testifies to You* that each and every word, statement and claim in this book is absolute, consistently verifiable and indisputable *TRUTH!*

If the Testimony of The Most High, Himself, isn't sufficient, *what would be?*

THE BRIEFINGS PRIOR TO AND AUDIENCE BEFORE THE MOST HIGH

STATEMENT OF CLAIM

Those words enscribed herein and indicated with double quote marks ("") **are given directly from The Most High** and translated and transcribed directly out of Angelic, the Language of All the Heavens Above All the Earths and in All the Depths Beneath All the Earths, **and are the Height of Absolute in Authority without exception.**

The Constitution of the United States as originally enacted is a Holy Document. The atrocities committed against it via court precedents; usually as (a) result of the victim not having financial resources to continue the necessary legal proceedings; and outright treasonous legislations enacted by One World Government socialists since its very inception, notwithstanding. Therefore:

1. **We, The Akurians, and Grand Marshal General Bobby Farrell, Et Al,** jointly and severally do hereby declare our respective rights thereunder, specifically but not limited to said rights as accorded under the provisions of the Bill of Rights, Amendment, the First, of what little remains of said Holy Document, The Constitution of the United States of America;

To Wit: "**Congress shall make no law respecting an establishment of religion, or prohibiting the free exercise thereof; or abridging the freedom of speech, or of the press; or the right of the people peaceably to assemble, and to petition the Government for a redress of grievances;**" thus we do hereby declare the establishment of this religion and the free and unencumbered voice thereof together with the publication of this work; in defiance of and despite the virtual now nonexistence of the aforesaid provisions of said Holy Document, The Constitution of the United States of America, including the proviso that we will not be bound by any statute or other requirement with respect to being 'politically correct' at any time nor under any conditions.

2. With respect to any and all content(s) hereof: **We, The Akurians, and Grand Marshal General Bobby Farrell, Et Al,** jointly and severally do hereby declare our respective rights as accorded under the provisions of Amendment, the First, Section 9, of what little remains of said Holy Document, The Constitution of the United States of America;

AKURIAN METAPHYSICAL HANDBOOK
VOLUME I

THE BRIEFINGS PRIOR TO AND AUDIENCE BEFORE THE MOST HIGH

INTRODUCTION

001. **If the Testimony of The Most High, Himself, isn't sufficient,** *what would be?* The sincere Seeker of Truth need only properly prepare themselves – which is a matter of Mind and Spirit and takes only a minute – to settle the issue forever. Seekers of Truth *do* need to *divest themselves of any and all previous programming*, be it ages old 'belief' or Demonic Doctrines of Death, usually the same thing, and not make any advance determinations. That The Most High, Himself, will *communicate directly with the individual* is a real cash-register rattler to all hallelujah halfwits, politicians, priests, preachers and other liars. Emblem of the Proven Knowers is below.

002. Because humans are so blatantly stupid, we suppose in ages past God could talk to designated entities, some of them humanoid, but has since lost the ability, the authority or just can't find anybody qualified with which to communicate. And with respect to what He calls ""That Great Babylonian Harlot at Rome and Constantinople,"" which includes all her Harlot Christian Daughters, the Nation of Islam, Hindu, Buddha and the rest of the world's religions, He doesn't! Especially since the outlawing and slaughter of the Gnostics – *Knowers* – by all the major 'religions.' Lucifer sends Demons in

all manner of disguises, but The Most High does not send anyone, except victims as a Testimony against them, to any of those religions. *YES!* He will Testify to that, too!

003.   As a result, there are few direct two-way conversations with The Most High, ancient or modern, found anywhere in the world including the Holy Bible, and none in modern times that can be verified beyond any question or doubt, *except these Akurian Volumes.*

004.   Adding to the crackpot assumption that God is of far lesser intellect and capability than man's Degrees in Theology, there is absolutely nothing recorded with respect to preparation for presenting one's self before The Most High. Neither names of those Entities who assisted in the past, nor what assistance they provided.

005.   This book calls all such smarter-than-God idiocies into account and presents a first-person transcript of which The Most High, Himself will Testify to its infallible truth and accuracy to any and all who will know these Divine Presents, *without* question.

006.   Suppression and outright slaughter of those who had, can and still do have such High Divinity Access are always victims of Demonic Elements, primarily religions, church- and Demon-dominated governments. The man of *this* Generation, of whom this Holy Script is given, is no exception in spite of the fact The Most High not only calls him into His Own Great Presence but Named His Own Name upon him! The Most High, Himself, confirms these

Audiences, His Own Holy Appointment upon this Beloved Son of Fire, and that each and every word, statement and claim in **"The ANOINTED, The ELECT, and The DAMNED!,"** is infinite, absolute, irrevocable, consistently verifiable Truth.

008. There are Holy Names, Identities, Great Elements (from which The Most High made all Creation), Eight Winds of the Ancient Mysteries, High Divinity Seraphim and their High Demon counterparts, Archangels and Angels all *correctly named* and some of them being invoked in these presents. They are called and directed in correct and proper order and procedure. Pronunciation is in parentheses following each, accent being noted by capital letters. Until you are proficient with these Names and totally devoid of all "praise Jesus," "hail Mary," "Allahu Akbar," white light and all other such abominations, *do not attempt* to use any of these entities or energies in any manner whatsoever.

007. For the sake of clarification only, throughout the entirety of this book, the Words of The Most High are in double quotes ("") and printed in Red; Seraphim and Angels in Royal Purple; and Supreme Lord of all High Lords El Aku ALIHA ASUR HIGH (General Bobby Farrell, photo below) is in Blue. Pronunciation is in brackets [] with the accent capitalized. Everything quoted in this presentation has been translated directly from Angelic, the Language of the Heavens, into English. Angelic is composed of untold colors, visuals and frequencies in addition to sounds that are beyond human voice capabilities. In the Planes of Heaven and Depths of

THE BRIEFINGS PRIOR TO AND AUDIENCE BEFORE THE MOST HIGH

Hell there is never a question of what is being presented in Angelic. The language is infinite in clarity and perfection.

009. A great world of Spiritual Truth, Knowledge and all its benefits awaits those who will divest themselves of their accrued and programmed Demonisms and venture into the Realms of Righteous Power and Holy Authority.

The Akurians.

Emblem of the Proven Knowers of
The Great Testimony,
those who have personally
experienced the unmistakable
Recognition of The Most High, Himself.
Actual width is Three US inches (3"), Gold.
The center is The Eye of The Most High
with thirteen sectors representing the actual
Thirteen Tribes of Israel.
The Name, AKU, is the short Title of this
Holy Order, The Akurians.

PRONUNCIATION

Most names are as spoken in **Angelic**,
the Language of the Heavens.
Accent is capitalized.

ALIHA ASUR HIGH [ah-LI-hah ASH-er high]
AKASHA [ah-KAUSH-ah]
Angel Holy Aniel [a-NI-EL]
Angel Holy Bahaliel [ba-HAL-e-EL]
Angel Holy Beli [BEL-i]
Angel Holy Forlok [FOR-lock]
Angel Holy Hamal [HAY-mile]
Angel Holy Jehuel [yeh-WHO-EL]
Angel Holy Nafriel [NAY-fri-EL]
Angel Holy Sarabotes [sar-a-BO-tes]
Archangel Gabriel [GAB-ra-EL]
Archangel Michael [MI-kal]
Archangel Raguel [RA-u-EL]
Archangel Raphael [RAF-a-EL]
Archangel Remiel [re-MI-EL]
Archangel Uriel [UR-e-EL]
Archangel Zerachiel [ZER-AK-e-EL]
ASUM DE AL HMONGA! [as-UM de al
 who-Mon-Ga – **All energies hear me / All
 energies hear us** – **Angelic**]
Ben Nez [ben-NEZ]
BHSAT! [beh-shat – **Completed in the Forever. / As
 it is spoken, so it is done!** – **Angelic**]
Cherubim Habha Hazhan [HAB-ba HAS-ann]
Danaka [da-NAH-kah – Second Depth of Hell]
Deros [DEE-ros – First Depth of Hell]
East Gate Pruel [pru-EL]

THE BRIEFINGS PRIOR TO AND AUDIENCE BEFORE THE MOST HIGH

East Wind Apelotes [a-pel-O-tees]
El Aku [L-AH-kou]
Fhisxrnt [hiz ZAX art]
Gehenna [geh-HEN-nah – Fourth Depth of Hell]
Hadesse [ha-DESS-ee – Third Depth of Hell]
HAKARMAH [hah-KAR-mah – Fifth Plane of Heaven]
Hapurdom [hah-PUR-dom – Sixth Depth of Hell]
HASANNAH [has-ANN-nah – Sixth Plane of Heaven]
HASTERAH [HAS-ter-ah – Second Plane of Heaven]
HATHOR [HAY-thor – First Plane of Heaven]
Heleeah [he-LEE-ah – Fifth Depth of Hell]
HESTERAH [HES-ter-ah – Third Plane of Heaven]
High Demon Abbadona [ah-bah-DO-nah]
High Demon Aeshmodeva [ash-mo-DAE-va]
High Demon Astarothae [as-TAR-oth, Iblis]
High Demon Baalberith [bal-BEER-eth]
High Demon Beelzebub [be-EL-zeb-ub]
High Demon Behemoth [be-HEM-oth]
High Demon Belphegor [BEL-fee-gor]
High Demon Forcas [FOR-cass]
High Demon Leviathan [le-VI-a-than]
High Demon Lucifer [LU-sah-fer]
High Demon Mammon [MAM-mon]
High Demon Shemhazai [shem-HA-zi]
High Demon Urakabarameel [ur-ak-a-BAR-ram-e-EL, HAK-KAR-ray-man]
High Demon Xaphan [ZA-fan]
IDEAH [ID-ee-ah – Fourth Plane of Heaven]
KESLATA [kes-la-tah – **That which the Lord hears must also be truth and righteous. – Angelic**]

North Gate Yhodukah [hew-du-KAH]
North Wind Boreas [BOR-us]
Perditon [per-DEE-ton – Seventh and Lowest Depth
  of Hell]
PZNIONA [piz-now-ona – **All is of the Lord as is
  inscribed. – Angelic**]
Qorqhus [KOR-gus]
Seraphim Amatraelonael [AM-at-ra-EL-ona-EL,
  Metatron]
Seraphim Jehoel [ye-HO-EL]
Seraphim Kemuel [KEM-u-EL]
Seraphim Nethanael [ne-THAN-a-EL]
Seraphim Ophaniel [OFF-an-e-EL]
Seraphim Seraphiel [ser-AF-e-EL]
Seraphim Zophiel [ZOF-e-EL]
Servant Wind Eurea [E-you-ah]
Servant Wind Kaikias [kay-KI-us]
Servant Wind Lipae [LI-pay]
Servant Wind Skiron [SKY-ron]
South Gate Albim [al-BI-m]
South Wind Notae [NO-tay]
VOAN [vone – **I have spoken before the Lord, and
  He has heard. – Angelic**]
West Gate Druiel [dru-e-EL]
West Wind Zephyros [zef-OR-a-ee]
YESHAMA DELIAH! [yeh-SHA-ma de-LIE-ah – **On
  my/our Authority – Angelic**]

THE BRIEFINGS PRIOR TO AND AUDIENCE BEFORE THE MOST HIGH

THE BRIEFINGS

010. The excerpts below are reduced to opening comments, as all the details and visuals in each commentary would take several thousand huge volumes in small print. Pay very close attention to the subject matter of each opening inquiry; each and every word, statement, recognition and question is of immense importance.

011. **Revelation 6:4** "And there went out another horse that was red: and power was given to him that sat thereon to take peace from the earth, and that they should kill one another: and there was given unto him a great sword."

10 January 2009 – 14 Tevet 5769

012. The Most High sent His Faithful Messenger Cherubim Habha Hazhan [HAB-ba HAS-ann] from His Presence to His Lord of Lords El Aku ALIHA ASUR HIGH, Second of the Great Horsemen, bivouacked with his Command at Qorqhus [KOR-gus] in the High Realm of Fhisxrnt [hiz-ZAX-art] in the High Abstracts, saying, "Prepare now for Audience before The Most High. Delay not. The Most High has summoned His Beloved Son of Fire to present yourself before Him to account that which you shall invoke upon the Earth according to your Holy Power and Righteous Authority from the now immediate unto Shiloh. Beloved Son of

Fire, be advised: the iniquity of the whole world is near to full."

013.   And I sent Cherubim Habha Hazhan on to the Supreme Council of the Seraphim of The Holy Presence to present my compliments and request audience and advisory for myself with respect to my Presentation. Cherubim Habha Hazhan completed his missions and returned to duty as Messenger of The Most High.

014.   In due order I was summoned and given permission to present myself before the Great Seraphim of The Holy Presence: Seraphim Amatraelonael [AM-at-ra-EL-ona-EL, Metatron], Chief of All The Holy Seraphim and Senior Lord of All Duty this side of the Great Veil; Seraphim Seraphiel [ser-AF-e-EL], Seraphim Jehoel [ye-HO-EL], Seraphim Kemuel [KEM-u-EL], Seraphim Nethanael [ne-THAN-a-EL], Seraphim Ophaniel [OFF-an-e-EL] and Seraphim Zophiel [ZOF-e-EL], the Supreme Grand Council of All Duty this side of the Great Veil. In presence were Archangel Raphael [RAF-a-EL], Ruler of the First Quarter of Air, Master of the East Wind Apelotes [a-pel-O-tees], Archangel Michael [MI-kal], Ruler of the Second Quarter of Fire, Master of the South Wind Notae [NO-tay], Archangel Gabriel [GAB-ra-EL], Ruler of the Third Quarter of Water, Master of the West Wind Zephyros [zef-OR-a-ee], Archangel Uriel [UR-e-EL], Ruler of the Fourth Quarter of Earth, Master of the North Wind Boreas [BOR-us], Archangel Remiel [re-MI-EL], Ruler of All the Binding in All the Heavens Above All the Earths, and in All the Earths, and in

THE BRIEFINGS PRIOR TO AND AUDIENCE BEFORE THE MOST HIGH

All the Depths Beneath All the Earths, Archangel Raguel [RA-u-EL], Ruler of the Loosening in All the Heavens Above All the Earths, and in All the Earths, and in All the Depths Beneath All the Earths, Archangel Zerachiel [ZER-AK-e-EL], First Guardian of All the Holy Anointed Witnesses in Their Generations. Each were in Company with their respective Immediate Staff as the affairs of the Heavens, the Earths and the Depths continue even as this Generation of Fire is scheduled to receive its Justification.

Grand Marshal General Bobby Farrell
"Getting Up To Nothing" CD Cover
Vandor International Records

AKURIAN METAPHYSICAL HANDBOOK
VOLUME I

Scripted from The Akashic Records
THE BRIEFINGS
14 January 2009 – 18 Tevet 5769

015. Seraphim Amatraelonael called the gathering to order and the Hosts to stand easy. I was stationed at the vantage and recognized for the proceedings.

016. Seraphim Amatraelonael: **"Son of Fire, Son of Fire, Beloved of The Most High, the hour has come that you must soon relieve your station. Prior to your relief it is incumbent that all the purposes of your assignment be fulfilled, even that sealed up until this Hour of Justification. This is the uppermost portion of your assignment. Are you prepared to proceed?"**

017. Lord El Aku: **"Sir!"**

018. Seraphim Seraphiel: **"Son of Fire, Son of Fire, Beloved of The Most High, the Children of Abraham in all the Earth have profaned themselves with the Canaanite in knowing violation of the Holy Statutes, defiling the blood and the souls of themselves and their generations after them. It is incumbent upon you to pronounce Justification upon all the Children of Abraham that shall not alter or remove from off any of them until Shiloh. Are you prepared to proceed?"**

019. Lord El Aku: **"Sir!"**

THE BRIEFINGS PRIOR TO AND AUDIENCE BEFORE THE MOST HIGH

020. Seraphim Jehoel: "Son of Fire, Son of Fire, Beloved of The Most High, the Children of Abraham in all the Earth have profaned themselves with the Cushite in knowing violation of the Holy Statutes, defiling the blood and the souls of themselves and their generations after them. It is incumbent upon you to pronounce Justification upon all the Children of Abraham that shall not alter or remove from off any of them until Shiloh. Are you prepared to proceed?"

021. Lord El Aku: "Sir!"

022. Seraphim Kemuel: "Son of Fire, Son of Fire, Beloved of The Most High, the Children of Abraham in all the Earth have profaned themselves with the Gentiles in knowing violation of the Holy Statutes, defiling the blood and the souls of themselves and their generations after them. It is incumbent upon you to pronounce Justification upon all the Children of Abraham that shall not alter or remove from off any of them until Shiloh. Are you prepared to proceed?"

023. Lord El Aku: "Sir!"

024. Seraphim Nethanael: "Son of Fire, Son of Fire, Beloved of The Most High, the Children of Abraham, even all Children of the Birthright in all the Earth have knowingly ostracized their own innate and blasphemed the Holy Spirit of Truth, defiling the blood and the souls of themselves and

their generations after them. It is incumbent upon you to pronounce Justification upon all the Children of Abraham that shall not alter or remove from off any of them until Shiloh. Are you prepared to proceed?"

025. Lord El Aku: "Sir!"

026. Seraphim Ophaniel: "Son of Fire, Son of Fire, Beloved of The Most High, the Children of Abraham, even all Children of the Birthright in all the Earth have knowingly followed after the Harlots of the Depths, defiling the spirits and the minds of themselves and their generations after them and all who heeded their damnations. It is incumbent upon you to pronounce Justification upon all the Children of Abraham that shall not alter or remove from off any of them until Shiloh. Are you prepared to proceed?"

027. Lord El Aku: "Sir!"

028. Seraphim Zophiel: "Son of Fire, Son of Fire, Beloved of The Most High, the Children of Abraham, even all Children of the Birthright in all the Earth have knowingly and with malice before The Most High expounded evil in all the World and have, at their own will and at their own hands, brought their own iniquity to full upon their own heads and upon all who could not escape their damnations. It is incumbent upon you to pronounce Justification upon all the Children of Abraham that shall not alter or remove from off

any of them until Shiloh. Are you prepared to proceed?"

029. Lord El Aku: **"Sir!"**

030. The Archangels brought forth the Akashic Records, the Book of Life, and revealed again all the details of those who did these damnations knowingly, and knowing the penalties for those violations. Yet the Levite Priests did them in knowing abuse of their powers of office, and the Chiefs of the House of Judah did them rejoicing in their greed. They had only to do the Holy Statutes and all would be well with them and their little ones generation after generation: there would be rain in due season; their crops would never fail; their women and livestock would never cast their young before the time; the land would flow with milk and honey; intelligence would abound; their enemies would keep themselves far from all Israel; there would be no plague come near their borders nor upon any house of Israel even at the farthest reaches; and there would be peace in all the land and wherever one of Israel should need to be.

031. From the Akashic Records I witnessed profanity upon profanity, unrepented of yet today, and now the iniquity is near to full and the Great Damnations are about to begin. In fact, they are already upon us: Kak (Ashkenazi) Jew to Kak Jew to Kak Jew in a never-ending Circle of Circumstance protecting all Ashkenazis and depriving everybody else. The current Federal Reserve System blackmail

of the United States and all the criminal financial activity being perpetrated overtly with layer upon layer of Kak Jew to Kak Jew to Kak Jew protection and legal immunity is but the beginning of sorrows. It was for this reason The Most High ordered and verified The Righteous Decree upon the Whole of the House of Levi and the Whole of the House of Judah, invoked June 1st, 2007 – 15 Sivan 5767, and The Irrevocable Curse of El Aku Upon The Whole of The House of Levi and The Irrevocable Curse of El Aku Upon The Whole of The House of Judah, invoked upon them again on June 27th, 2007 – 11 Tamuz 5767 (after sunset, 12 Tamuz 5767).

032.   Do not be deceived by the appearance of Canaanites in the Ashkenazi Jew-Controlled media. Every Jew knows the Prophets: **Zechariah 14:21 – ""... And in That Day there shall be no more the Canaanite in the House of the Lord of Hosts!""** When the Canaanites have served their purpose they will be executed simply because they are Canaanites; and one cell of Canaanite blood will be sufficient to qualify for extermination. The fact the House of Ephraim (United States) put a soulless half-breed, accursed Canaanite in the Office of President is compounded by the fact he, and all his staff and appointees, are Marxists: the most damnable and Demonic of all philosophies.

033.   Seraphim Amatraelonael called the gathering and the Hosts to stand down, ordering the gathering and their Hosts to assemble again, establishing the availability.

THE BRIEFINGS PRIOR TO AND
AUDIENCE BEFORE THE MOST HIGH

Scripted from The Akashic Records
THE BRIEFINGS
15 January 2009 – 19 Tevet 5769

034. Seraphim Amatraelonael called the gathering to order and the Hosts to stand easy. I was stationed at the vantage and recognized for the proceedings.

035. Seraphim Amatraelonael: "Son of Fire, Son of Fire, Anointed Warrior of The Most High, it is declared unto you that because of the Abominations, the whole world must suffer its due; it is declared unto you that the Instigators and Inciters of all the Abominations are the Whole of the House of Judah in conspiracy with the Whole of the House of Levi, since the Day of Abandonment of the Holy Ark of the Testimony. Are you prepared to receive that truth?"

036. Lord El Aku: "Sir!"

037. Seraphim Seraphiel: "Son of Fire, Son of Fire, Anointed Avenger of The Most High, it is declared unto you that in the Day of Abandonment of the Holy Ark of the Testimony, all the House of Israel were in ignorance save the High Priests of Levi and the Chiefs of all the families of the House of Judah. The whole of the House of Levi became a House of Desecrated Spirit, and the Whole of the House of Judah became a House of Insatiable Greed. By signs and wonders it was given unto the Whole of the Houses of Israel concerning the

Displeasure and the Wrath of The Most High, and there were repentances, but the House of Levi never again presented themselves as fully righteous before The Most High, and the House of Judah never again presented themselves as divested of immense greed. And they are both yet this day merciless and consider not the devastation upon their own Tribe in their lust for wealth and the power of wealth. Are you prepared to receive that truth?"

038.   Lord El Aku: "Sir!"

039.   Seraphim Jehoel: "Son of Fire, Son of Fire, Anointed Destroyer of The Most High, it is declared unto you that in the Day of Abandonment of the Holy Ark of the Testimony, the Day of Abandonment of the Holy Ark of the Testimony should have been the Day of Great Accomplishment, securing The Great Testimony unto all the Children of Abraham and unto all the Tribes of All the Gentiles that there is a True and Most High God in the Heavens who is ever mindful of all His Creations, even unto the farthest reaches of Creation. For this cause were the Righteous always chosen, even Abraham being pure in his generations; and his children have abandoned him and his Righteousness. Are you prepared to receive that truth?"

040.   Lord El Aku: "Sir!"

041. Seraphim Kemuel: "Son of Fire, Son of Fire, Anointed Supreme Priest of The Most High, it is declared unto you that in the Day of Abandonment of the Holy Ark of the Testimony, all the Heavens did mourn and Lucifer and all his minions rejoiced. Yea, while the Heavens and all the Hosts of Heaven mourned, Lucifer and all his minions rejoiced, for they had been invited by the Whole of the House of Judah and sanctified in the Whole of the House of Levi. Are you prepared to receive that truth?"

042. Lord El Aku: "Sir!"

043. Seraphim Nethanael: "Son of Fire, Son of Fire, Anointed Supreme Priest of The Most High, it is declared unto you that in the Day of Abandonment of the Holy Ark of the Testimony, the way was set and has not been unset for all mankind to know both the Everlasting Majesties of The Most High and His Untellable Wrath. Yea, for the Everlasting Majesties are of endless mercy upon the truly repentant, and His Untellable Wrath is unending upon all who make themselves His enemies; for whosoever truly serves is repentant and whosoever violates is an enemy. Are you prepared to receive that truth?"

044. Lord El Aku: "Sir!"

045. Seraphim Ophaniel: "Son of Fire, Son of Fire, Anointed Supreme Judge of The Most High, it is declared unto you that in the Day of

Abandonment of the Holy Ark of the Testimony, there was Fire in all the Heavens as testimony against the Whole of the House of Levi and the Whole of the House of Judah that they repent and do not this evil upon themselves, their generations after them and the whole world to come. But they would not. That unholy few set forth to make themselves senior to all others, even Israel and the whole world; and they have not removed that intention from themselves unto this day. Are you prepared to receive that truth?"

046. Lord El Aku: "Sir!"

047. Seraphim Zophiel: "Son of Fire, Son of Fire, Anointed Supreme Teacher of True Righteousness of The Most High, it is declared unto you that in the Day of Abandonment of the Holy Ark of the Testimony, it was presented unto the Whole of the House of Jacob, even Israel, that all had been fulfilled and accomplished in accordance with the Holy Statutes: that all the world would see The Presence of The Most High and a Holy People to present access to all Righteousness. And the Whole of the House of Jacob, even Israel, was deceived by the Levite Priests of the Inner Court and Jews of the Outer Tabernacle that the Abandonment was not known even to the other Priests nor all Israel, and the whole world is yet deceived of it. Are you prepared to receive that truth?"

THE BRIEFINGS PRIOR TO AND AUDIENCE BEFORE THE MOST HIGH

048.   Lord El Aku: "Sir!"

049.   The Archangels brought forth the Akashic Records, the Book of Life, and revealed all the details of those who did these damnations knowingly, and knowing the penalties for those violations. And those Akashic Records revealed the Day of Abandonment of the Holy Ark of the Testimony was planned and executed as part of a scheme to make acceptable sacrifices available for a price by Judean merchants set up just outside the Tabernacle and along the Tabernacle accesses.

050.   The idea was for the Levite Priests to accept the same sacrificial livestock over and over again that the Judean merchants could sell the same livestock over and over again in direct and knowing violation of the Holy Statutes, because The Most High would know and would certainly execute the High Priest on the next Day of Atonement when he was required to enter, clean the area and make certain sacrifices as prescribed by Holy Statute. The only alternative was to NOT enter the Holy of Holies, and to do that required the collusion of the other Tabernacle Priests who were present in the inner court. The secret must not even be known to the other Levite Priests who were not present, and then only to those who were found to be acceptable to the extra money the scam accorded.

051.   There had been ample warning for such disobedience with the death of Aaron's two sons, Nadab and Abihu, for using unclean fire. Things really came to a head when the Israelites and

Midianites encamped near to one another, and Israel fell into whoredom with the Midianites: racemixing, eating sacrifices to Midianite gods, the entire list of Abominations forbidden by Holy Law. Then when the iniquity of Israel was full, The Most High commanded Moshe to put things back in order with a plague of executions that killed twenty-four thousand and hung their heads out in the sun where nobody was going to miss the display nor misunderstand the reason for it.

052. Even with all these signs, warnings and sufferings for disobedience, Israel, enticed by Judah and approved by Levi, time and time again the entire Nation fell into punishment for angering The Most High. Now, the United States (Ephraim) and the rest of the world are in the same kind of mess for the same reason, and the worst is yet to come. I am personally going to see to it.

053. Seraphim Amatraelonael called the gathering and the Hosts to stand down, ordering the gathering and their Hosts to assemble again, establishing the availability.

The Akurian's Political Opinion!

THE BRIEFINGS PRIOR TO AND AUDIENCE BEFORE THE MOST HIGH

Scripted from The Akashic Records
THE BRIEFINGS
16 January 2009 – 20 Tevet 5769

054. Seraphim Amatraelonael called the gathering to order and the Hosts to stand easy. I was stationed at the vantage and recognized for the proceedings.

055. Seraphim Amatraelonael: "Son of Fire, Son of Fire, High Lord Anointed of the Generations of Ish, know The Most High Lord of Spirits will inquire of your Final Intentions concerning the Whole of the House of Levi, who has profaned the Great Righteousness unto Eternal Damnation. Are you prepared to know the full extent of those damnations and do Justice in The Sight of The Most High?"

056. Lord El Aku: "Sir!"

057. Seraphim Seraphiel: "Son of Fire, Son of Fire, High Lord Anointed of the Generations of Ish, know The Most High Lord of Spirits has not changed anything of Himself nor anything of His Holy Statutes, nor will there be any changes whatsoever until all be fulfilled. The Age of Great Tribulations must come before the Age of Great Restoration as given by the Holy Prophets. Are you prepared to know the full extent of those damnations and do Justice in The Sight of The Most High?"

058. Lord El Aku: "Sir!"

059. Seraphim Jehoel: "Son of Fire, Son of Fire, High Lord Anointed of the Generations of Ish, know The Most High Lord of Spirits has not surrendered His Great Powers of Great Miracles nor the Righteous Processes of them: all such Righteous Processes being defiled by the Whole of the House of Levi in their desecrations. Are you prepared to know the full extent of those damnations and do Justice in The Sight of The Most High?"

060. Lord El Aku: "Sir!"

061. Seraphim Kemuel: "Son of Fire, Son of Fire, High Lord Anointed of the Generations of Ish, know the Days of Temptation by Lucifer having been fulfilled, The Most High Lord of Spirits has determined the ending of Days of Tolerance: upon the Whole of the House of Levi who sold the Righteousness, first; upon the Whole of the House of Judah who spare not to degenerate, second; upon the Socialists who encourage the Canaanites and cause them to deny the Great Curse upon themselves, third; upon the Canaanites and all who tolerate them in their degeneracies, fourth; and upon the House of Ephraim and the House of Manasseh, who are the Birthright of Israel before The Most High, in all their damnations. Are you prepared to know the full extent of those damn-

ations and do Justice in The Sight of The Most High?"

062. Lord El Aku: "Sir!"

063. Seraphim Nethanael: "Son of Fire, Son of Fire, High Lord Anointed of the Generations of Ish, know the Days of Tribulation are now irrevocable, and in the Fury of The Most High Lord of Spirits the Days of Terror and Deprivation are soon to be upon the whole world, and those under authority of the Corrupt of the House of Judah, the Demon Possessed of That Great Babylonian Harlot at Rome and all Islam shall be in danger of their own thoughts. Are you prepared to know the full extent of those damnations and do Justice in The Sight of The Most High?"

064. Lord El Aku: "Sir!"

065. Seraphim Ophaniel: "Son of Fire, Son of Fire, High Lord Anointed of the Generations of Ish, know the Days of Holocaust are now irrevocable, and in the Fury of The Most High Lord of Spirits the Days of Horror are soon to consume the whole world. Though liars deny and fools believe them, Russia and China **(communists)** are a greater part of the evil; they shall not escape the agonies they seek to inflict to rule the world. Are you prepared to know the full extent of those damnations and do Justice in The Sight of The Most High?"

066. Lord El Aku: "Sir!"

067. Seraphim Zophiel: "Son of Fire, Son of Fire, High Lord Anointed of the Generations of Ish, know the Days of Justification are now irrevocable, and the Fury of The Most High Lord of Spirits must be satisfied. There are not sufficient Righteous in the whole world that The Lord Most High will spare the world for their behalf. Are you prepared to know the full extent of those damnations and do Justice in The Sight of The Most High?"

068. Lord El Aku: "Sir!"

069. The Archangels brought forth the Akashic Records, the Book of Life, and revealed all the details of those who did these damnations knowingly, and knowing the penalties for those violations. Among the most abominable is That Great Babylonian Harlot at Rome, the Roman Empire now in disguise as a 'religion,' who schemed to permit the people one *dead* Messiah rather than any *living* Messiah in their own generation. They did not, and still do not, hesitate to murder as many as necessary to enforce their Demonic edicts; confiscating, suppressing, editing and forging scriptural writings, 'canonizing' those that ensured their absolute power while permitting a few deemed irrelevant to their plans, mostly Ancient Prophets, thrown as bones to those who would resist. In actual 'religious' practice they spared neither sword nor hardships to achieve

a totally 'catholic' world ruled from Rome. The absolutely unspeakable atrocities they committed against Native Americans are on par with any abominations in the entire history of mankind including the psychopathic abominations of the Nation of Islam whom The Most High refers to as, *"The Unholy Vipers of Perditon."*

070. Now that the Fury of The Most High Lord of Spirits is irrevocable, the energies of all the damnations of Levites, Judeans, Marxists, Communists, Fascists, Socialists and the fools who support them in all their treasons, concocted wars and openly public scams are about to manifest in more hardships than civilization has ever seen before, and cannot survive. The Kak Jew Socialist stranglehold of the Rothchilds, Rockefellers and Bilderbergers is so complete, even the communist countries with all their total enslavements cannot resist any whims Kak Jew Socialists want to impose upon them.

071. Do not misunderstand: the House of Levi and the House of Judah created, financed, published, expounded and enforced Marxism, dividing it into two reputedly opposing philosophies – communism and fascism – to exploit the profits from the wars instigated between them, and the wars instigated to establish their respective forms of government upon the citizenry wherever and whenever the opportunity presented itself. If there wasn't an available opportunity for such instigated wars of 'liberation,' the House of Levi and the House of Judah created the opportunity.

072. Do not misunderstand: Ashkenazis of the House of Levi and the House of Judah will pay any price, even defiling their own children into race-mixing, to gain power and control over a Tribe, a People or a Nation. They will spare nothing to infest and infect the very fiber of the foundations until they gain their stranglehold over the whole of the people and the government, from the most menial labor to the highest offices they can manipulate from behind the scenes with as much secrecy as possible.

073. The House of Levi and the House of Judah have done this in every country since the Diaspora following the conquest of Judea and destruction of Jerusalem by the Romans in the late First Century. The Ashkenazis turned it into a real art form after 'converting' to Judaism in the 7th Century. In spite of the failures and the slaughters of untold millions of their Ashkenazis, Levite and Judean fellows when their treasons came to light upon demanding payment-in-full for a debt they themselves had made unpayable – just like the bailouts abounding around the world today – they gathered the survivors together and, just like today, whined their innocence and nonexistent righteousness as "the chosen children of god" wherever they could stay long enough for anybody to listen ... and always to the listener's misfortune and eventual destruction.

074. Seraphim Amatraelonael called the gathering and the Hosts to stand down, ordering the gathering and their Hosts to assemble again, establishing the availability.

THE BRIEFINGS PRIOR TO AND AUDIENCE BEFORE THE MOST HIGH

Scripted from The Akashic Records
THE BRIEFINGS
17 January 2009 – 21 Tevet 5769

075. Seraphim Amatraelonael called the gathering to order and the Hosts to stand easy. I was stationed at the vantage and recognized for the proceedings.

076. Seraphim Amatraelonael: "Son of Fire, Son of Fire, Holy One of the Children of Abraham, it has come before The Most High that the end of Abominations and Atrocities by all the Tribes, by all the Peoples and by all the Nations is Justified and your Hour of Justification is even now. We are instructed of The Most High to direct you that you should spare not the Whole of the House of Levi and the Whole of the House of Judah even as you shall spare not the Houses of the Heathen, Marxists, Communists, Fascists, Socialists, Progressives, Democracies, Republics, Dictatorships and Monarchies. Are you prepared to know the extent of their Damnations that you make sure and certain Justification upon them and all their generations after them unto Shiloh?"

077. Lord El Aku: "Sir!"

078. Seraphim Seraphiel: "Son of Fire, Son of Fire, Holy and Righteous Son of the Children of Abraham, we are required of The Most High to direct you that of all the Tribes yet upon the whole world there is none more unrighteous in The Sight

of The Most High than the Tribe of Levi; and our Testimony is against them. When you called to the whole world to repent and return to the Holy Statutes, the House of Levi set forth to scorn you first, and they have not spared to ensure your deprivation and defamation. We are directed to comfort you in your knowing The Most High is His Own Testimony against the Whole of the House of Levi for their unending deprivations, abuses and defamations against you and your Holy Office. Are you prepared to know the extent of the House of Levi's Damnations that you make sure and certain Justification upon them and all their generations after them unto Shiloh?"

079. Lord El Aku: "Sir!"

080. Seraphim Jehoel: "Son of Fire, Son of Fire, Holy and Righteous Son of the Children of Ishmael, we are required of The Most High to direct you that of all the Tribes yet upon the whole world there is none more vile in The Sight of The Most High than the Tribe of Judah; and our Testimony is against them. When you called to the whole world to acknowledge the conspiracies of the House of Judah toward their control of all commerce and information, the House of Judah did not spare to curse you in all their services nor to announce all degeneracy against you. We are directed to comfort you in your knowing The Most High is His Own Testimony against the Whole of the House of Judah for their unending conspiracies

against you and your Holy Office. Are you prepared to know the extent of the House of Judah's Conspiracies that you make sure and certain Justification upon them and all their generations after them unto Shiloh?"

081.   Lord El Aku: "Sir!"

082.   Seraphim Kemuel: "Son of Fire, Son of Fire, Holy and Righteous Son of the Children of Isaac, we are required of The Most High to direct you that of all the Tribes yet upon the whole world there are none more deceived in The Sight of The Most High than the Tribe of Ephraim and the Tribe of Manasseh; and therefore our Testimony is against the United States of America and the United Kingdom of Britain. Since the beginning of the Days of Damnation in 5598 **(1838 GCAD)** by Karl Heinrich Marx, financed, published, supported and expounded by the House of Levi and the House of Judah in knowing conspiracy against the whole world, neither Ephraim nor Manasseh drew out their swords against them lest their own little ones be entrapped and enslaved, as they were called upon to do by the Holy Statutes. Yea, even in this day when you call upon the whole world to repent and return to the Holy Statutes you are scorned and rebuked by the House of Ephraim and the House of Manasseh who dare neither speak against nor in any manner resist the Damnations of the Marxists, because the Damnations of the Marxists are the breath and blood of the Whole of

the House of Levi and the Whole of the House of Judah. Are you prepared to know the extent of the deceptions against the House of Ephraim and the House of Manasseh that you make sure and certain Justification upon them and all their generations after them unto Shiloh?"

083.   Lord El Aku: "Sir!"

084.   Seraphim Nethanael: "Son of Fire, Son of Fire, Holy and Righteous Son of the Children of Jacob, we are required of The Most High to direct you that of all the Tribes yet upon the whole world there are none more violent in their Damnations Against Themselves upon the whole world than the Tribes of Ishmael; and thus our Testimony is against them. And when you presented their Kings, Ayatollahs, Grand Imams and their Universities with full access to all The Most High gave unto you to present, and without cost save their own effort to observe, they did each and all ignore your invitation and The Summons of The Most High; and thus is our Testimony of them. When you called to all the Children of Abraham and to the whole world to repent and return to the Holy Statutes, none ignored you more than the Tribes of Ishmael, bent on violence and conversion to Islam by the Sword. Yea, The Most High is His Own Testimony against the Whole of the Tribes of Ishmael for their unending neglect against you and your Holy Office. Are you prepared to know the extent of the Tribes of Ishmael's Damnations

Against Themselves that you make sure and certain Justification upon them and all their generations after them unto Shiloh?"

085. Lord El Aku: "Sir!"

086. Seraphim Ophaniel: "Son of Fire, Son of Fire, Holy and Righteous Son of the Children of Joseph, we are required of The Most High to direct you that of all the Tribes yet upon the whole world there are none more vile nor violent in their lust for immediate power of wealth upon the whole world than the Tribes of China; and our Testimony is against them. You have called to the whole world to repent and return to the Holy Statutes, to reject all House of Levi and House of Judah supported and endorsed naming Marxism, Communism, Fascism and Socialisms. You have been scorned and rebuked by all those of public information sources leaving the whole world in ignorance, and their own murders at the hands and whims of the Socialists are accounted upon their own heads as they are accounted upon the Whole of the House of Levi and the Whole of the House of Judah and all their accomplice Socialists. Yea, The Most High is His Own Testimony against the Whole of the House of Levi and the Whole of the House of Judah for all these unending abuses and defamations against you and your Holy Office. Are you prepared to know the extent of the desecrations of righteousness, atrocities, murders and iniquities of Marxism, Communism, Fascism,

Socialism and China that you make sure and certain Justification upon them and all their generations after them unto Shiloh?"

087.   Lord El Aku: "Sir!"

088.   Seraphim Zophiel: "Son of Fire, Son of Fire, Holy and Righteous Son of the Children of David, we are required of The Most High to direct you that of all the Tribes yet upon the whole world there are none more deceitful nor more dishonest in their lust for total power over the whole world than the Tribes of Russia; and our Testimony is against them. You have called to all the living innates upon the whole world to repent and return to the Holy Statutes, to reject all House of Levi and House of Judah supported and endorsed Damnations of Deceit: Marxism, Communism, Fascism, Socialism and Progressivism. You have been scorned and rebuked by all government authorities, all publications and all gatherings to their own detriment and deceit of the whole world. You have called to the whole world to repent and return to the Holy Statutes, and you have been denied, defied, defamated, robbed, restricted, scorned and rebuked more by the House of Levi and the House of Judah than all the rest of the world combined; even more than That Great Babylonian Harlot at Rome and all her Harlot Christian Daughters. Are you prepared to know the extent of the Tribes of Russia's Damnations of Deceit given unto them by the House of Levi and

> the House of Judah that you make sure and certain Justification upon them and all their generations after them unto Shiloh?"

089. Lord El Aku: "Sir!"

090. The Archangels brought forth the Akashic Records, the Book of Life, and revealed again all the details of those who did these damnations knowingly, and knowing the penalties for those violations. I saw conspiracy upon conspiracy formulated at the family table, at the office, at the resort, at the park, at the scenic view, at the lodge, at the closed conference, at the synagogue, at the pre-conventions, at the conventions, at the elections, at the government agencies, at the pre-trial conferences, in the courts and at all the offices of power. There wasn't any place where Levites, Jews, Politicians or Bureaucrats, especially and specifically Ashkenazis who call themselves Jews and are not, gather that such collusions and conspiracies toward Global Marxism were not matters of course.

091. And everywhere the Levite and the Jew were foremost in instigation and leadership of the legislated enslavements.

092. The conspiracies and collusions were as rampant as the words of the perpetrators, ensuring that whosoever should be in the public sight could not deviate from the dictates of the House of Levi and the House of Judah and their Global Marxist intentions, regardless of the abomination and regardless of the damnation. Wherever it seemed

necessary to strengthen the Circle of Circumstance – Kak Jew to Kak Jew to Kak Jew to Kak Jew – they spared no effort or taxpayers' money to remove any patriot and install their own puppet, from the lowest service counters to the management desks to the highest conference tables.

093. Seraphim Amatraelonael called the gathering and the Hosts to stand down, ordering the gathering and their Hosts to assemble again, establishing the availability.

**Command Marshal General D. Chylon Budagher, P.K.
Grand Council of Gnostics 2005-2010, 2010-2015
Command Executive Officer**

**THE BRIEFINGS PRIOR TO AND
AUDIENCE BEFORE THE MOST HIGH**

Scripted from The Akashic Records
THE BRIEFINGS
18 January 2009 – 22 Tevet 5769

094. Seraphim Amatraelonael called the gathering to order and the Hosts to stand easy. I was stationed at the vantage and recognized for the proceedings.

095. Seraphim Amatraelonael: "Son of Fire, Son of Fire, Holy and Righteous Anointed Witness of the Generation of Fire, know The Most High has sent you to a vile and morally bereft generation not of their own making but of the deliberate deprivation of truth, knowledge and understanding by the Whole of the House of Levi and the Whole of the House of Judah and the incarnated minions of Lucifer [LU-sah-fer]: Abbadona [ah-bah-DO-nah], Aeshmodeva [ash-mo-DAE-va], Astarothae [as-TAR-oth, Iblis], Baalberith [bal-BEER-eth], Beelzebub [be-EL-zeb-ub], Behemoth [be-HEM-oth], Belphegor [BEL-fee-gor], Forcas [FOR-cass], Leviathan [le-VI-a-than], Mammon [MAM-mon], Shemhazai [shem-HA-zi], Urakabarameel [ur-ak-a-BAR-ram-e-EL, whose Title in Angelic is HAK-KAR-ray-man] and Xaphan [ZA-fan]. They are a vile and morally desolate company. Are you prepared of them against the Day of Reckoning?"

096. Lord El Aku: "Sir!"

097. Seraphim Seraphiel: "Son of Fire, Son of Fire, Holy and Righteous Anointed Witness of the

Generation of Fire, know The Most High has sent you to a vile and violent, power-mad, morally bereft, spiritually degenerate and Demon-possessed generation that refuses to look, knowing it would observe its own degeneracies. And all the Great and Fallen left alive are against you unto their own destruction and have ordered the Infernal Lords of Eternal Damnation to spare not even the deepest Depths of Hell to destroy you, all Akurians and all those seeking True Righteousness. Are you prepared of them against the Day of Reckoning?"

098.   Lord El Aku: "Sir!"

099.   Seraphim Jehoel: "Son of Fire, Son of Fire, Holy and Righteous Anointed Witness of the Generation of Fire, know The Most High has sent you to an ignorant and stupid generation whereof the abominations of the House of Levi and the damnations of the House of Judah, the peaceful restoration of the Holy Statutes is as a blaspheme and a desecration to the Whole of the Tribes, the Whole of the Peoples and the Whole of the Nations. Are you not reviled by every soul professing the calling of Muhammad, even the greater Sons of Ishmael? Are not their Demons everywhere and spare not against you? Are you prepared of them against the Day of Reckoning?"

100.   Lord El Aku: "Sir!"

**THE BRIEFINGS PRIOR TO AND
AUDIENCE BEFORE THE MOST HIGH**

101. Seraphim Kemuel: "Son of Fire, Son of Fire, Holy and Righteous Anointed Witness of the Generation of Fire, know The Most High has sent you to a jealous and profane generation whereof the whole world is vile and profaned within their very souls. The Soul of Israel and the Soul of Ishmael are jealous and profane in their minds; and the Soul of the Gentiles is desecrated with the Demons of Socialism. Are you not reviled by every soul professing the calling of Judaism, even the greater Sons of Aaron? Are not their Demons everywhere and spare not against you? Are you prepared of them against the Day of Reckoning?"

102. Lord El Aku: "Sir!"

103. Seraphim Nethanael: "Son of Fire, Son of Fire, Holy and Righteous Anointed Witness of this Generation of Fire, know The Most High has sent you to the Whole of the House and the Tribes of Shem, and the Whole of the House and the Tribes of Abraham, and the Whole of the House and the Tribes of Ishmael, and the Whole of the House and the Tribes of Israel; and the Whole of the House and of the Tribes of Japheth, and the Whole of the Houses and the Tribes of the Gentiles; and the Whole of the House and the Tribes of Ham, even the Whole of the House and the Tribes of Canaan and the Whole of the House and the Tribes of Cush: and at their own invitation are they all possessed by Demons. Thus do they continue under all manner of lies and Demonic deceptions

to murder and to slay many innocent that a few may live in power and in luxury, and their deceits and damnations have contaminated the whole world. Are you not reviled by every soul professing the calling of Jesus, even the greater men and women of that Blasphemy? Are not their Demons everywhere and spare not against you? Are you prepared of them against the Day of Reckoning?"

104. Lord El Aku: "Sir!"

105. Seraphim Ophaniel: "Son of Fire, Son of Fire, Holy and Righteous Anointed Witness of the Generation of Fire, know The Most High has sent you to a putrid, corrupt and murderous generation; and our Testimony is against them for there is no righteousness found anywhere among them. Beware! First, beware of all Judah; for they are a jealous, lying, greedy and profane people without honor or integrity, even in their Synagogues where all Levi supports them. Second, beware of all Levi, for with all their pretended righteousness they are a living abomination unto all truth and unto all True Spirit. Third, beware of all Ishmael; for they are a Demon-possessed and murderous lot, bent only on murder for the sake of murder under the guise of righteousness. Fourth, beware of That Great Babylonian Harlot at Rome and all her Harlot Christian Daughters; for those among them are no lesser an evil than the Demons who possess them. And none of them shall spare anything

under their hand to destroy you and yours, whether a lying word or an entire generation of their firstborn. Such is their determination of the Demons. Are you not reviled by every soul professing their own righteousness in their own ignorance? Are not their Demons everywhere and spare not against you? Are you prepared of them against the Day of Reckoning?"

106. Lord El Aku: "Sir!"

107. Seraphim Zophiel: "Son of Fire, Son of Fire, Holy and Righteous Anointed Witness of the Generation of Fire, know The Most High has sent you to a stupid and mentally incognizant generation of their own making: A speechless and dumb generation programmed into ignorance that they see and hear and know not; that they do, and harm themselves and learn not; for such is the Leavening of the Damned. And all the Damned are of Lucifer and his minions, even the Whole of the House of Levi in their desecrations and the Whole of the House of Judah in their abominations in The Sight of The Most High. The Demons of Socialism are the same Demons of That Great Babylonian Harlot at Rome and all her Harlot Christian Daughters, and the Righteous Truth concerning them is no longer hidden from the Tribes, the Peoples and the Nations; thus they are without excuse. Are you not reviled by every soul professing his own Agenda of Socialist Demonisms? Are not their Demons everywhere and spare

not against you? Are you prepared of them against the Day of Reckoning?"

108.   Lord El Aku: "Sir!"

109.   The Archangels brought forth the Akashic Records, the Book of Life, and revealed again all the details of those who did these damnations knowingly, and knowing the penalties for those violations. Though the degeneracies began in the Ages of the Nefilim, who set forth the most vile and degenerate examples of conduct in direct and knowing violation of Holy Law, the High Servants of the Anusazi (Servants of Anu) preached morality and obedience to Holy Law and privately practiced the degeneracies of the Nefilim.

110.   The lineage of Ish (Adam, Adama) were the most righteous, and for the most part kept their generations pure, especially the lineage of the Birthrights. After Noah invoked the Great Curse on Canaan, Canaan and Cush conspired to thwart The Most High by mixing their Tribes – which failed in its entirety as all "Big Nigger" scenarios do – nothing was spared by the descendants of Canaan and Cush to breed themselves out from under the Great Curse of Noah. Racemixing was declared holy, righteous, permissible and to none effect by Semiramis (the *first* 'mother of god'), lying about her pregnancy with Nimrod, fathered by her Uncle Cush. The Levites, Jews, That Great Babylonian Harlot at Rome and all her Harlot Christian Daughters practice and

endorse that degeneracy to this day, 2009 **(GCAD)**. Marxists promote the same Abomination of Abominations to expand a soulless and easily programmed ignorant generation of fools to people their wars, created disasters and legislated enslavements.

111.   The average person, not knowing the majorities they must adhere to *are soulless,* nor that Holy Law is both unchanged and forbids racemixing of any kind, are easy prey for the damnations of the Doctrines of Death and the Demons of Socialism. They follow willingly into the depths of depravity, believing the lies, voting known criminals to govern them, glorifying the practices of degeneracy and praising those who intend eventual enslavement and slaughter upon them and their generations after them.

112.   And so it is that truth is treason and Holy Law is blasphemy in their minds, their governments and in all their courts. And so it also is that their own tribulations (troubles) of plagues, famines, enslavements and merciless death are soon to be upon them all – *without exception* – and accounted upon their own heads and at their own hands. Nevertheless, their abominations, degeneracies and troubles be damned: they have Blasphemed the Holy Office of The Most High, the Holy Office of the Anointed Witness and Messiah in this living generation, and I will not pass it without full repentance and due compensation.

113. Seraphim Amatraelonael called the gathering and the Hosts to stand down, ordering the gathering and their Hosts to assemble again, establishing the availability.

Shoulder Ensigna, King's Regiment,
Military Order of Pathfinders.
All Commissioned Officers are Ordained.
Pathfinders must be self-supporting
and cannot live off their Congregations.

THE BRIEFINGS PRIOR TO AND AUDIENCE BEFORE THE MOST HIGH

Scripted from The Akashic Records
THE BRIEFINGS
19 January 2009 – 23 Tevet 5769

114. Seraphim Amatraelonael called the gathering to order and the Hosts to stand easy. I was stationed at the vantage and recognized for the proceedings.

115. Seraphim Amatraelonael: "Prince of War, Prince of War, Supreme High Priest of All High Priests, Holy and Righteous Messiah of the Generations of Ish, know The Most High has declared the Day of Shiloh of the Judgments, the Years of Desolation and of Tribulation and the Ages of Restoration, even the hour when Lucifer shall be bound by Lord Immanuel and escorted of the Great Horsemen into The Pit of Darkness. Know that Lord Lucifer and all his minions are fully aware their time is short unto Shiloh, and they shall spare not to turn each and every soul to their Damnations or destroy the whole world that there be none alive, even the Elect of The Most High. Are you prepared to engage and defeat Lord Lucifer in these last times of his great fury?"

116. Lord El Aku: "Sir!"

117. Seraphim Seraphiel: "Prince of War, Prince of War, Supreme High Priest of All High Priests, Holy and Righteous Messiah of the Generations of Ish, know The Most High has directed us to inform you of the means and manners of Lord Lucifer and

his minions and the conspiracies and collusions of the Whole of the House of Levi, the Whole of the House of Judah, That Great Babylonian Harlot at Rome and all her Harlot Christian Daughters to rule the whole world in the name of Lord Lucifer or destroy even the Very Elect of The Most High. Know that Lord Lucifer has made currency and coin of the realm into a flaming sword, cutting and destroying even when sheathed. The Great Sword of National Destruction came into consideration in 5538 **(1778 GCAD)** and was instituted by Lord Lucifer and his minions in 5551 **(1791 GCAD)** as part of the Protocols of the 500 Year Plan of the House of Levi and the House of Judah. They will not surrender the replacement Federal Reserve System without many lies and much bloodshed. Are you prepared to engage and defeat Lord Lucifer in these last times of his great fury?"

118.   Lord El Aku: "Sir!"

119.   Seraphim Jehoel: "Prince of War, Prince of War, Supreme High Priest of All High Priests, Holy and Righteous Messiah of the Generations of Ish, know The Most High has directed us to inform you the current global financial situation is the direct end result of the precepts given in The Protocols of the Learned Elders of Zion, being but one chapter in the 500 Year Plan, and this day are each and every precept thereof the laws and practices of the Whole of the lands of Ephraim, the United States, First Half of Israel; and Manasseh,

United Kingdom, Second Half of Israel. The Protocols of the Learned Elders of Zion include the new sword, the United States Federal Reserve System, and those precepts are soon to be the Marxist Legislation of the United Nations toward the economic enslavement of the whole world. They will not surrender the replacement Federal Reserve System without many lies and much bloodshed, nor will they ever admit the truth that The Protocols of the Learned Elders of Zion are true and but one guidebook in the Grand Plan of TOTAL Global Enslavement. Are you prepared to engage and defeat Lord Lucifer in these last times of his great fury?"

120.   Lord El Aku: "Sir!"

121.   Seraphim Kemuel: "Prince of War, Prince of War, Supreme High Priest of All High Priests, Holy and Righteous Messiah of the Generations of Ish, know The Most High has directed us to inform you the current global financial situation is not the natural result of market and resources. It is the end result of decades of Marxist Manipulations by the Whole of the House of Levi and the Whole of the House of Judah against the righteous interests of both Ephraim and Manasseh and the whole world, that their elite few should rule and command from the stations of wealth. Know the patience of Demons exceeds the patience of Saints; but the patience of Lucifer is at an end because he knows his remaining time is short, and he shall be

consumed in his own fire at your hand. The Demon-possessed Socialists will not surrender the replacement of the Internal Revenue Service without many lies and much bloodshed, nor will they ever admit the truth of their Manipulation by those dedicated to one solitary control of all that exists upon the earth. Are you prepared to engage and defeat Lord Lucifer in these last times of his great fury?"

122.   Lord El Aku: "Sir!"

123.   Seraphim Nethanael: "Prince of War, Prince of War, Supreme High Priest of All High Priests, Holy and Righteous Messiah of the Generations of Ish, know The Most High has directed us to inform you the current social enmities upon the whole world are of the spirits of evil, even the Demons of Socialism treading their easy way in the wake and aftermath of That Great Babylonian Harlot at Rome and all her Harlot Christian Daughters, being manipulated over the millennia by the Whole of the House of Levi after the elect Priesthood sold the Righteousness and by the Whole of the House of Judah in their greed. Yea, the Great Curse of Noah is upon the Whole of the Tribes of Canaan, and the Greater Curse of The Most High is upon the Whole of the Tribes of Cush. But the greater of the Abominations is upon the Whole of the House of Levi and the Whole of the House of Judah, for they have not repented unto any Holy and Righteous Messiah of the

Generations of Ish; neither have they turned from their own damnations upon their own head. The abandonment of truth by the followers of Santana Dharma, the eternal law, permitting the loss of knowledge of the Nefilim shall not go unaccounted; and the abandonment of the Ancient Ways by Islam is equal in its evil. Thus these six sewers: the Demons of Socialism, being first since its inception; the sacrifices of men, women and children by That Great Babylonian Harlot at Rome and blasphemes of all her Harlot Christian Daughters; Abominations of the House of Levi and Damnations of the House of Judah; the Great Curses upon all of Canaan and upon all of Cush; the abandonment of truth by the Hindus; and the massive murdering of the innocents by the Children of Ishmael, are of equal liability in The Sight of The Most High. The Demons have done well with them, for they will spare not to destroy all who shall expose them by Truth and by Righteousness, and their fools will follow and obey. Are you prepared to engage and defeat Lord Lucifer in these last times of his great fury?"

124.   Lord El Aku: "Sir!"

125.   Seraphim Ophaniel: "Prince of War, Prince of War, Supreme High Priest of All High Priests, Holy and Righteous Messiah of the Generations of Ish, know The Most High has directed us to inform you that all the current wars and violent conflagrations between the Families, the Tribes, the

Peoples and the Nations are not of righteousness seeking justice, but are of manipulations of the Demons of Religions, and the Demons of Socialism, and the Demons of the Whole of the House of Levi and the Whole of the House of Judah. Many the wars and many the dead and many the harmed and suffering at the hands of the Whole of the House of Levi and the Whole of the House of Judah that the Levite and the Jew be enriched and empowered of wealth by those wars of division. Yea, the House of Levi and the House of Judah infest and infect the affairs of all others that they befriend the unwary; to instigate animosity between the unwary of one and the unwary of another and lend great sums to both; one for swords and arrows and the other for shields and buckler; and not that either unwary should prevail quickly, but that the wars should extend and extend and extend and extend, that the Levite and the Jew profit for generations. The Demon-possessed of the Whole of the House of Levi and the Whole of the House of Judah will not surrender their offices and institutions of power to create war and control money without many lies and much bloodshed, nor will they ever admit the truth of their Manipulations clearly seen by all who will venture to observe. Are you prepared to engage and defeat Lord Lucifer in these last times of his great fury?"

126.   Lord El Aku: "Sir!"

THE BRIEFINGS PRIOR TO AND AUDIENCE BEFORE THE MOST HIGH

127.   Seraphim Zophiel: "Prince of War, Prince of War, Supreme High Priest of All High Priests, Holy and Righteous Messiah of the Generations of Ish, know The Most High has directed us to inform you that all the great statutes and all the great institutions of mankind are scheduled for the Wrath of the Fire and the Fury of The Most High at your leisure. The national extortions committed by the Whole of the House of Levi and the Whole of the House of Judah by their conspiracies, collusions, manipulations of their Marxisms, Communisms, Fascisms, Socialisms and their legal and economic espionages to destroy the Great Constitution and the economic and moral fabric of Freedom, Liberty and Justice shall not escape the death's edge of your Great Sword: for it is the Will of The Most High. The whole of the House of Levi and the Whole of the House of Judah, already in collusion with That Great Babylonian Harlot at Rome and her many Harlot Christian Daughters, financial institutions of the Children of Ishmael and the Demonic Governments of Communism shall not spare you in their anger at being exposed to all who will venture to observe. Lucifer will not spare any of the Fallen nor their minions nor any of the possessed to destroy you in the Face of Holy Truth that they further intimidate the Tribes, the Peoples and the Nations. Are you prepared to engage and defeat Lord Lucifer in these last times of his great fury?"

128.   Lord El Aku: "Sir!"

129. The Archangels brought forth the Akashic Records, the Book of Life, and revealed again all the details of those who did these damnations knowingly, and knowing the penalties for those violations. I had but one small surprise, the inclusion of the Hindus for their failure to maintain the knowledge before the public that all the history they have is of the Nefilim, the *"watchers"* of the Hebrew Bible. The Hindus should have made that history clear and public to the whole world rather than absorb it as a religion. A very small and easily corrected situation, but one that must be corrected lest the thousands of years of suffering because of that error come down upon the Hindus and the neglected alike in these Days of Justification.

130. I was not surprised by anything else in either the briefings or the presentations. There is nothing else new therein to the observant. Those who ***will not*** see cannot see of their own blindness and are stupid because they will not correct their own ignorance. Ignorance of spiritual things, political things, economic things and even life and health things are the same as ignorance of the law in any court: ignorance of the law is no excuse. And none, not even the churches, religions and political organizations who profess a great deal of lies and damnations from their temples, mosques, synagogues, lodges and offices are going to be excused for so much as one iota of that which they did that should not have been done, nor anything they did not do that should have been done. Rather than their self-glorifications in the names of gods, prophets and the

people, they should be far more concerned with their own accounting of their evils in the name of Righteousness when they are required to confront the Great Sword given me and the Righteous Power and Holy Authority to take peace from the earth. For mine will not be for profit nor control, but for the fulfillment of the Days of Horror and the Years of Tribulation of the Wrath of The Most High.

131.   Seraphim Amatraelonael called the gathering and the Hosts to stand down, ordering the gathering and their Hosts to assemble again, establishing the availability.

THE AKURIANS PRAYER

(Hands open, palms up) "ALIHA ASUR HIGH, hear your servant(s). I/We am/are humble in The Presence of The Ancient of Days. My/Our voice is quiet in the great roar of Creation. All I/we ask is to be found worthy of candidacy for Citizenship in The Kingdom of God, and that You have already granted. All Righteous Power and Holy Authority be upon Your Avenger, El Aku ALIHA ASUR HIGH."

THE AKURIANS BLESSING

(Hand out and over the person/object) "El Aku, Hah-Kan-Nah. [hah-KAN-nah]" Translates in English to "Aku Bless You." "Hahkannah" is a word in Angelic that encompasses many levels of heavens, depths, realms, souls, spirits, minds, things, meals, water, drink, weather, land, nations, ships, et cetera, and even graveyards when spoken by the True Righteous. Spoken by anybody else, it's a three syllable word bereft of any power whatsoever.

AKURIAN METAPHYSICAL HANDBOOK
VOLUME I

Scripted from The Akashic Records
THE BRIEFINGS
20 January 2009 – 24 Tevet 5769

132. Seraphim Amatraelonael called the gathering to order and the Hosts to stand easy. I was stationed at the vantage and recognized for the proceedings.

133. Seraphim Amatraelonael: "**Lord of Lords El Aku ALIHA ASUR HIGH, Supreme Anointed Witness of The Most High, Supreme Lord of Vengeance of The Most High, Holy and True is your Testimony against the Whole of the House of Ephraim in this Great Damnation; Holy and True is your Testimony against the Whole of the House of Manasseh in their Great Damnation; Holy and True is your Testimony against the Whole of the House of Levi and their Abominations against all Righteousness and against the whole world; Holy and True is your Testimony against the Whole of the House of Judah and their Damnations against all Righteousness and against the whole world; Holy and True is your Testimony against the Whole of the House of Ishmael and against all Islam for their wholesale murder of innocents in disguise of holy service; Holy and True is your Testimony against the Whole of the House of Canaan and against the Whole of the House of Cush and their defilements and contaminations of the whole world seeking to remove the Righteous Curses from off themselves; Holy and True is your Testimony against That Great Babylonian Harlot at**

Rome and against all her Harlot Christian Daughters and all their blasphemes against The Most High and His Holy Law; Holy and True is your Testimony against all their conspiracies, collusions, intrigues, murders, suppressions and coverups, and Holy and True is your Testimony of their attempts to incarcerate, detain, silence and defame you and the Holy Office of Living Anointed Messiah in their own generation. Supreme Lord Avenger of The Most High, are you prepared to unsheathe your Great Sword and draw it out against all the mentioned enemies of The Most High?"

134.   Lord El Aku: "Sir!"

135.   There was an instant silence in the gathering as recognition of The Most High came to be.

**Battle Ensign of the Second Horseman,
El Aku ALIHA ASUR HIGH**

AKURIAN METAPHYSICAL HANDBOOK
VOLUME I

INTERVENTION FROM THE MOST HIGH

136. ""Holy and Righteous Son of Fire, spare not the whole world for the Abominations committed in the sight of the whole world this Day in Ephraim. Holy and Righteous Son of Vengeance, spare not the whole world for the Damnations committed in the sight of the whole world this Day in Ephraim. Holy and Righteous Prince of War, spare not the whole world for the Desecrations committed in the sight of the whole world this Day in Ephraim. Ephraim has declared the soulless Canaanite to be their chief over them in all the land; therefore, because they have preferred the decadence of Canaan and the depravity of Cush and the abominations of Levi and the damnations of Judah, I have declared the Great Curses upon Canaan, Cush, Levi and Judah to be upon the Whole of the House of Israel and all the Tribes and Houses thereof. First upon the Abominable House of Levi and upon the Damnable House of Judah; and upon the House of Joseph, My Birthright, even Ephraim and Manasseh, upon whom My Servant Jacob named his own name Israel; and all I have permitted of the Great Curses and all I have demanded in the Great Curses shall be upon the Whole of the land. And I will not repent of My Punishment and My Wrath upon any who have perpetrated these damnations upon themselves and their fellows, neither will I prevent nor mollify the sufferings upon the Whole of the

citizenry, for they have brought forth My Wrath and I will not spare until Shiloh.

137. ""Holy and Righteous Lord of My Vengeance, spare not the whole world for the Defamations against Truth, against Righteousness, against Freedom, against Liberty and against Justice done in the sight of the whole world this Day in Washington **(District of Columbia)** at the hands of all Ephraim. For they aggrandize themselves sitting in the seats of great power, but they shall scream in great agony unto Me when you send them to sit in the lowest seats of hell. Know, Beloved Son of My Eternal Vengeance, that I will not hear them in these hours nor in the hours of their destruction, neither they nor any of their generations after them. Unto whomsoever you shall Judge against, I shall hear not until Shiloh.

138. ""Holy and Righteous Lord of My Great Wrath, spare not the whole world for the Damnations of My Holy Statutes against all mankind done in the sight of the whole world this Day in the Great City of Great Corruptions and Great Conspiracies and Great Treasons. For Ephraim has lifted a possessed of Lucifer to be all power over them, which should not be done anywhere among the Children of My Servant Abraham.

139. ""Holy and Righteous Horseman of My Great Enlightenment, you call yourself a sinner before me, but I call you Righteous before me. Unto you was given by earned right the Office of Supreme King of War in the face of Lucifer, The

Satan, and a Great Sword and Righteous Powers and Holy Authorities and a Great Lance of Fire that in That Day none can stand against you and survive. By that which you have earned and by that which I have seen to bestow upon you, spare not My Wrath and My Vengeance upon the whole world and all the generations thereof until Shiloh.

140. ""Holy and Righteous Anointed Messiah of the Generations of Ish, the Whole of the House of Levi has profaned the whole world; the Whole of the House of Judah has desecrated the minds of the whole world; and between them they have sown war, plague, drought, famine, disease and the Death of the Soul with That Great Babylonian Harlot at Rome and her Harlot Christian Daughters. Spare them not.

141. ""Holy and Righteous and Worthy Son of Abraham, the Tribes of Ishmael have defaulted their righteousness and betrayed their share of the Birthright before My Face; for I do not require, neither do I entice, nor do I bless, the slaughter of any innocent. I am not a God of lies and weakness that I must be gathered to by the sword or by starvation. I reward not any with heavenly steeds, nor with harems of wives, neither do I present domiciles of great opulence, for My Rewards are greater than that and none suffer to deliver it or to have or to hold or to possess it forever. Therefore the Children of the Tribes of Ishmael who have played the harlot of abominations of Beelzebub are a cess before Me, and I order you to spare them not.

**THE BRIEFINGS PRIOR TO AND
AUDIENCE BEFORE THE MOST HIGH**

142. ""Holy and Righteous Son of My Pride, send forth unto every eye that will see and unto every ear that will hear and unto every tongue that will speak, that: This Day have I declared the Great Curse of Canaan upon the Whole of the House of Ephraim, even the United States, and I shall not remove it until there is no more the Levite nor the Judean found anywhere in power in the Whole of the House of Joseph. Proclaim unto all who will heed, that: This Day have I declared the Great Curse upon Cush upon the Whole of the House of Ephraim, even the United States, and I shall not remove it until there is no more the Canaanite in the House of Joseph. Whosoever shall learn of these presents and repent without exception shall you put up your Great Sword and withdraw your Great Lance and invoke not any word against them and their generations after them. But whosoever shall deny these presents: spare them not.

143. ""Holy and Righteous Lord King of Kings of Israel, this Day am I blasphemed in Ephraim in the sight of the whole world. This Day is the first day of the fulfillment of the iniquities of the Whole of the House of Levi, the Whole of the House of Judah, the Whole of the Tribes of Canaan, the Whole of the Tribes of Cush, the Whole of the Tribes of the Children of Ishmael and the Whole of the Tribes of the Houses of Israel, and the Whole of all the Tribes of the Gentiles. This is not the Abomination of Desolation spoken of by My Servant Daniel during the Great Exile; but it is a Great Abomination before Me and a Great

AKURIAN METAPHYSICAL HANDBOOK
VOLUME I

Abomination against Me. Therefore I Command of you: spare them not.""

END OF THE INTERVENTION BY
THE MOST HIGH.

The Most Powerful Spiritual Book Ever written.
The Equivalent of the Christian Bible, Muslim Qur'an
and Bhagavad Gita, combined!

THE BRIEFINGS PRIOR TO AND AUDIENCE BEFORE THE MOST HIGH

144. Seraphim Amatraelonael directed continuance of our proceedings without comment. The Most High did not spare His Fury at having a soulless Canaanite sitting in the highest seat of Ephraim!

145. Seraphim Seraphiel: "Lord of Lords El Aku ALIHA ASUR HIGH, Supreme Anointed Witness of The Most High, Supreme Lord of Vengeance of The Most High, Holy and True is your Testimony against the Levites, the Jews, the Muslims, the Catholics, the Christians, the Canaanites, the Cushites, the Marxists, the Communists, the Fascists, the Socialists, the Foreign Interests and the unworthy and self-ignorant citizens who this day bring down upon their own head, upon all the Tribes, upon all the Peoples, upon all the Nations and upon the whole world and upon all the generations of the whole world until Shiloh: which Great Abomination and Damnation should not have been done before The Face of and in defiance of The Most High; justifying even the Great Curse of Noah upon Canaan, the Great Curse of The Most High upon Cush, the Penalties of the Holy and Righteous Decree on the 1st Day of June, 2007 **(GCAD)** – 15 Sivan 5767, the Irrevocable Curse of El Aku upon the Whole of the House of Levi and the Irrevocable Curse of El Aku upon the Whole of the House of Judah on the 27th Day of June, 2007 **(GCAD)** – 11 Tamuz 5767 **(Hebrew)**. Supreme Lord Avenger of The Most High, are you prepared to unsheathe your Great Sword and draw it out

against all the declared enemies of The Most High?"

146. Lord El Aku: "Sir!"

147. Seraphim Jehoel: "Lord of Lords El Aku ALIHA ASUR HIGH, Supreme Anointed Witness of The Most High, Supreme Lord of Vengeance of The Most High, Blessed is he that comes with The Name of The Most High named upon him. We have seen you in the Heavens, in the Earths and in the Depths beneath the Earths, and have seen you in The Holy Presence of The Most High where we too serve our Holy Stations. We are directed to inform you of the great mysteries of the great damnations now rampant upon the whole world. We shall not call the extortions of the Nation by those within the Nation any good thing, nor less than the knowing abomination upon the people, and the knowing blasphemes against the Holy Spirit of Truth, and knowing violations of the Holy Statutes by any other name or title. We declare unto you the parable of a penny. Whereof a penny was brought forth as the value of a penny, and that penny was the true worth of a true penny; it was brought forth for investment for profit in its time and safekeeping. And those to whom were brought the penny took it and said of it to ten others, "this is a penny, do with it as you will" and each of that ten went forth proclaiming they each had a penny of true value and worth. And each of that ten went forth to another ten and presented

themselves as having a penny of true value and worth; but value of that penny as true value and worth of that penny was yet a penny; there were now one hundred and ten claims of value and worth upon that penny. Those who went forth proclaiming they each had a penny, save the owner of the penny and the one to whom the penny was brought for investment and safekeeping, knew the penny was but one penny and knowingly proclaimed that one penny to be of full value and worth. And when that one hundred of the first ten set their claims of that one penny to yet another ten like themselves, the one penny appeared to have the value and worth of a thousand pennies. Yet the value and the worth of all their endeavors was but one penny, and all the rest was knowingly false and fraudulent. And thus it is with the United States Federal Reserve System: a knowing fraud without integrity, without honor, and without any honesty; a deception and a crime and a knowing abomination in The Sight of The Most High. Supreme Lord Avenger of The Most High, are you prepared to unsheathe your Great Sword and draw it out against all the declared enemies of The Most High?"

148.   Lord El Aku: "Sir!"

149.   Seraphim Kemuel: "Lord of Lords El Aku ALIHA ASUR HIGH, Supreme Anointed Witness of The Most High, Supreme Lord of Vengeance of The Most High, know the treasons against the

Whole of Ephraim and the Whole of Manasseh, even the Birthright House of Joseph, even Israel, are not blood and bones of foreign Tribes and Peoples and Nations, but are blood and bones of the Birthright House of Joseph who have defiled themselves with the whoredoms of other gods and the desecration of their own clear thought of mind. The traitors within the Birthright House of Joseph, even Israel, are knowing traitors with malice aforethought and great worshiping of the Demons of Socialism and the Demons of That Great Babylonian Harlot at Rome and all her Harlot Christian Daughters. The traitors within the House of Joseph have not ceased since their inception, and they will not cease until the Demons of Death claim them once they have served all their purposes. Do not spare to require the Demons of Death upon them – for they slay not as the Angels of Death – but deliver the Souls of the Damned unto Hapurdom **[hah-PUR-dom]** where they burn until Final Judgment. Spare them not, for the souls of the millions they have caused to die in their wars and of their manufactured diseases who should not have died cry forth from the grave and Realms of the Dead unto you for Justice; and this is the Hour of Justification. Supreme Lord Avenger of The Most High, are you prepared to unsheathe your Great Sword and draw it out against all the declared enemies of The Most High and the Birthright House of Joseph, all the Houses of Abraham and all the Tribes of the Gentiles?"

THE BRIEFINGS PRIOR TO AND AUDIENCE BEFORE THE MOST HIGH

150. Lord El Aku: "Sir!"

151. Seraphim Nethanael: "Lord of Lords El Aku ALIHA ASUR HIGH, Supreme Anointed Witness of The Most High, Supreme Lord of Vengeance of The Most High, know the traitors of the Birthright House of Joseph, even Jacob, even Israel, are not and never were innocent in their manipulations against the Freedom, Liberty and Justice of the Peoples or the Nation; and their manipulations against the economic welfare of the Whole of the Birthright House of Joseph – and the whole world – are by design and intended to destroy the economies and break the spirit of the people. Since 5538 **(1778 GCAD)** when it became known to the Whole of the House of Levi and the Whole of the House of Judah there would be a Nation not of Kings and That Great Babylonian Harlot at Rome, but of Freedom, Liberty and Justice in spite of the Harlot Christian Daughters who would infuse their spiritual pollutions, there came the recognition that wealth-for-lend would not be eliminated upon demand for payment by expulsion and slaughter of Levites and Jews to void the debt as it had been for generations of Kings and That Great Babylonian Harlot at Rome. That it was their brother's house, even the Birthright House of Joseph and Israel, they would spoil to achieve control of all wealth and mastery over all the living did not deter them from such desecration of Holy Statutes nor destruction of their own brother. Supreme Lord Avenger of The Most High, are you

prepared to unsheathe your Great Sword and draw it out against all the declared enemies of The Most High and the Birthright House of Joseph, all the Houses of Abraham and all the Tribes of the Gentiles?"

152.   Lord El Aku: "Sir!"

153.   Seraphim Ophaniel: "Lord of Lords El Aku ALIHA ASUR HIGH, Supreme Anointed Witness of The Most High, Supreme Lord of Vengeance of The Most High, know the desecration and destruction of all learning in the House of Joseph is not of greater technology or higher social requirement; neither is the failure of all learning in the House of Joseph by conditions beyond control of the people. The entire failure of all learning in the House of Joseph is by deliberate design of the Demons of Socialism; even the Whole of the House of Levi and the Whole of the House of Judah accompanied by those who have inflicted themselves with the Great Demons of Disaster unto wholesale tyranny against themselves and all their generations after them. They are all without excuse in The Sight of The Most High. The agenda of the traitors in the House of Joseph was and still is to infest and infect as much ignorance unto stupidity into the rising generation that they desecrate themselves and see not their planned extermination, and to require much expense for things abominable to bankrupt and destroy the economy and economic stability of the House of

Joseph unto its own destruction. The Whole of the House of Levi and the Whole of the House of Judah, the Whole of the Nation of Islam, the Whole of the Congregations of That Great Babylonian Harlot at Rome, the Whole of all the Harlot Christian Daughters, the Whole of all the Lodges and Gatherings of Conspiracy would flee as debris in the wind before the storm should the people awaken themselves and rise up in indignation. And thus too, they are all without excuse in The Sight of The Most High, for they love the enemies who eat their children. Supreme Lord Avenger of The Most High, are you prepared to unsheathe your Great Sword and draw it out against all the declared enemies of The Most High and the Birthright House of Joseph, all the Houses of Abraham and all the Tribes of the Gentiles?"

154. Lord El Aku: "Sir!"

155. Seraphim Zophiel: "Lord of Lords El Aku ALIHA ASUR HIGH, Supreme Anointed Witness of The Most High, Supreme Lord of Vengeance of The Most High, know the desecration of morality and putrification of the youth are not limited to the House of Joseph, but are global objectives perpetrated by the Whole of the House of Levi and the Whole of the House of Judah, the Whole of the Nation of Islam, the Whole of That Great Babylonian Harlot at Rome and all her Harlot Christian Daughters, serving the Demons of Socialism, Marxism, Communism and Fascism. They have

perpetrated these abominations in The Sight of The Most High knowingly and with malice aforethought. Therefore they are without excuse in The Sight of The Most High. Holy and true is your Testimony against the Whole of the House of Levi and the Whole of the House of Judah and the Whole of That Great Babylonian Harlot at Rome and all her Harlot Christian Daughters when they whine their innocence: claiming love for all, toleration of abominations, desecration of True Spirit and damnations upon all who reject and resist their labels of liberalism. For these are they who brought forth the disasters of narcotics; pollution of pure bloodlines by racemixing; degradation of entertainment; the importation of subcultures to destroy the purity of the Nations; desolation of honesty and integrity in all levels of government and commerce; devastation of peace, safety and order from the highways and the cities unto the very roots and foundations of the people; the knowing poisoning of all food, husbandry, farming and water sources. And they are all without excuse in The Sight of The Most High. Supreme Lord Avenger of The Most High, are you prepared to unsheathe your Great Sword and draw it out against all the declared enemies of The Most High and the Birthright House of Joseph, all the Houses of Abraham and all the Tribes of the Gentiles?"

156. Lord El Aku: "Sir!"

THE BRIEFINGS PRIOR TO AND
AUDIENCE BEFORE THE MOST HIGH

157. The Archangels brought forth the Akashic Records, the Book of Life, and revealed again all the details of those who did these damnations knowingly, and knowing the penalties for those violations. Nothing that has befallen the whole world since not later than 1788 **(GCAD)** except natural disasters of fire, flood, earthquakes and volcanic eruptions has been as result of either accident or normal life energies and pressures. Nothing. Each and every war, epidemic, plague, famine, ethnic cleansing, crime wave, financial recession and financial depression has been brought about by the Grand Plans of the Elders of Zion, which includes the Whole of the House of Levi and the Whole of the House of Judah in disguise of Liberalism, Marxism, Communism, Fascism and Socialism, in political and financial collusion with the Catholic Church and as many hallelujah halfwit Christians as could be duped into servitude to their own destruction.

158. The Fury of The Most High is directed toward all of them, and neither the other Children of Abraham nor the Tribes of the Gentiles are going to escape their share of the punishments. When I take peace from the earth, I will not exempt any of them except the True and Righteous Akurians in all the remaining generations until Shiloh. Do not misunderstand. Do not be deceived. I will exempt only the True and Righteous Akurians and their generations who are True and Righteous Akurians of themselves and in their own earned right. Nobody else. Nobody. None. I am going to set forces in motion to deliver wars upon wars; epidemics upon epi-

demics until there is a pox on every house in all of Levi and in all of Judah and upon all their fellows; plagues upon plagues so rampant the carnivores will prey upon one another rather than consume human cadavers; famines upon famines so severe that one's own dung will be a delicacy; crime waves upon crime waves that the perpetrators shall fare no better than the victims; ethnic cleansing and racial strife that whoever does the slaughter will assume they are doing God a favor; financial recessions and depressions so severe the Levite and the Jew and the Socialist will serve up their own family members as raw swine for a cup of urine or a pinch of dung; horrors upon horrors so many and so great that death will seem a relief; terrors upon terrors so many and so great those in the day will pray for night and those in the night will pray for sunrise; disasters upon disasters so many and so great that every priest, preacher and other liars will curse their own Demonic Damnations because they cannot bring relief; and destructions upon destructions so many and so extreme that generations will seek shelter thinking to stay for only a moment and not remember the location.

159. And these are the True and Righteous Judgments; and I will deliver them on all the generations from the Great Curse of Canaan upon the United States until Shiloh. That all socialism is of Demons and the Degenerate, and the soulless liar who now sits in the Seat of the President is both a communist and a One World Government traitor, will not exempt any who are responsible for his being there –

including the voters – from their share of condemnation in Judgment. That said, I am going to remove all their ilk from all offices of power and influence whatsoever.

160. Seraphim Amatraelonael called the gathering and the Hosts to stand down, ordering the gathering and their Hosts to assemble again, establishing the availability.

THE HOLY MARK OF GOD

Everybody has heard of the "Mark of the Beast" spoken of in the Book of Revelation 13, 14, 15, 16, 19 and 20; but very few have heard of the Holy Mark of The Most High spoken of in Ezekiel 9:4-6.

Ezekiel 9:4 And the Lord said unto him, Go through the midst of the city, through the midst of Jerusalem, and set a mark upon the foreheads of the men that sigh and that cry for all the abominations that be done in the midst thereof.

Ezekiel 9:5 And to the others he said in mine hearing, Go ye after him through the city, and smite: let not your eye spare, neither have ye pity:

Ezekiel 9:6 Slay utterly old and young, both maids, and little children, and women: but come not near any man upon whom is the mark; and begin at my sanctuary. Then they began at the ancient men which were before the house.

The Holy Mark of The Most High can only be presented by The Most High! In this Generation of Ish, it is sealed in the forehead of those who experience The Great Testimony.

There is no amount of 'belief' or other such hogwash that will deliver The Holy Mark of The Most High; His Power, His Authority, His Acceptance. Instant life-style changes are required, and obedience to Holy Law, all of which are given in "The ANOINTED, The ELECT, and The DAMNED!"

AKURIAN METAPHYSICAL HANDBOOK
VOLUME I

Scripted from The Akashic Records
THE BRIEFINGS
21 January 2009 – 25 Tevet 5769

161. Seraphim Amatraelonael called the gathering to order and the Hosts to stand easy. I was stationed at the vantage and recognized for the proceedings.

162. Seraphim Amatraelonael: "Son of Abraham, Son of Isaac, Son of Ishmael, Son of Jacob, Son of David, El Aku ALIHA ASUR HIGH, Living Anointed Son of The Most High Lord of All Spirits, know that though the earth is your possession, it is become a sewer in all its surface elements and a cess of degeneracy of all the Peoples throughout the whole world; and all its detriments are by design of the Elders of the House of Levi and the Elders of the House of Judah in collusion with That Great Babylonian Harlot at Rome and the abject, contagious ignorance of all her Harlot Christian Daughters. No less guilty is the Nation of Islam, who seek not any righteous example to call souls to the Name of Allah, but seek only the swords of violence to murder for the sake of murder. Thus they are and thus they are seen in The Sight of The Most High. Set what price you deem for the desecration of your earth and the putrification of your world; for The Most High has seen it righteous to make the whole earth and all its inhabitants the sole and exclusive possession of His Holy Anointed

Messiahs in their respective Reigns; and you may do what you will with that which is your own."

163. Lord El Aku: "Sir!"

164. Seraphim Seraphiel: "Son of Abraham, Son of Isaac, Son of Ishmael, Son of Jacob, Son of David, El Aku ALIHA ASUR HIGH, Living Anointed Son of The Most High Lord of All Spirits, know there are enemies upon the earth set to possess the whole world unto its total destruction. The greatest of enemies are but four. Marxism, Communism, Fascism in all their appearances of Grand Socialism are but one, and they are of the same Demons and of the same Damnations. That Great Babylonian Harlot at Rome and all her Harlot Christian Daughters in all their disguises of appearance of True Religion are but one, and they are of the same Demons and of the same Damnations. The Nation of Islam in all its several sects of Muslims are but one, and they are of the same Demons and of the same Damnations, possessed of Beelzebub and his minions. The whole of the House of Levi and the Whole of the House of Judah are but one, and they are of the same Demons and of the same Damnations, and are the greatest of all the four enemies of the earth, the whole world, and all mankind. And these four are the source and substance of Lucifer's powers and doctrines upon the earth and throughout the whole world."

165. Lord El Aku: "Sir!"

166. Seraphim Jehoel: "Son of Abraham, Son of Isaac, Son of Ishmael, Son of Jacob, Son of David, El Aku ALIHA ASUR HIGH, Living Anointed Son of The Most High Lord of All Spirits, know that mankind himself is not totally innocent, even in his victimization and the deceits perpetrated upon him for generations. Man is not totally innocent. In the very beginning of life of each and every soul The Most High established a pure and righteous innate that none should be deceived nor ignorant except they so choose of themselves. None can be so suppressed of ignorance that their innate be unable to make known that which is evil and that which is righteous, save they be insane. Therefore, even the Gentiles are not totally innocent even in the deceits and deprivations forced upon them. How much less then, the Children of Abraham? and the Whole of the House of Levi, who were given access to all Righteousness? and the Whole of the House of Judah, who were given the Septre of Identification of Israel? and the Whole of the House of Joseph, even Ephraim and Manasseh, who were given the Birthright of Jacob? and the Whole of the House of Ishmael, who were given the Princes? No, innocence is not found anywhere of Ishmael or Isaac or the Gentiles."

167. Lord El Aku: "Sir!"

THE BRIEFINGS PRIOR TO AND AUDIENCE BEFORE THE MOST HIGH

168. Seraphim Kemuel: "Son of Abraham, Son of Isaac, Son of Ishmael, Son of Jacob, Son of David, El Aku ALIHA ASUR HIGH, Living Anointed Son of The Most High Lord of All Spirits, know that of all disasters found anywhere in the world, whether social, political or religious, none are of themselves and all are of deliberate design and manipulation. Even hardships in the wake of earthquakes and mighty storms are exacerbated by the Marxist, Communist, Fascist, Socialist and manipulators of the House of Levi and the House of Judah. Know that the Elders of Levi will expend all other Levites and all Jews and all Gentiles, and the Elders of Judah will expend all other Jews and all Levites and all Gentiles for the sake of the power of a single penny. Thus they are and thus they are seen in The Sight of The Most High. Let not their whinings of their innocence deceive any Akurian, for they have no innocence anywhere in all the House of Levi nor anywhere in all the House of Judah. Whosoever will be deceived let them be deceived. Upon the whole earth and everywhere in the whole world there is neither upheaval nor hardship that is not the direct end result of the Socialist manipulations of the Elders of the House of Levi and the Elders of the House of Judah. Whosoever will be deceived let them be deceived, for the losses are accounted upon their own head and at their own hand. Know that the Elders of Levi and the Elders of Judah are the Elders of Zion, and the claim of 'learned' is but a self-glorification and a bait unto all the foolish."

169. Lord El Aku: "Sir!"

170. Seraphim Nethanael: "Son of Abraham, Son of Isaac, Son of Ishmael, Son of Jacob, Son of David, El Aku ALIHA ASUR HIGH, Living Anointed Son of The Most High Lord of All Spirits, know the greater glories and accomplishments of man shall not be until after Second Judgment, and never under the Demons of Socialism. Know there shall be no great deliverer in all the ages of man until after Shiloh and the Great and Final Judgment. Know there are already many pretenders, and many followers seeking their own ascension to the Throne of Power and the Thrones of Glory at the fall of the current pretender. Know that in all these evils The Voice of The Teacher of Righteousness and your True Disciples shall not go entirely unheard nor unheeded. There shall be a few. There shall be only a few who seek Truth, True Righteousness and The Living God ALIHA ASUR HIGH. There shall be only a few of the generations of the True and Righteous Akurians, where a very few is more than enough to declare The Most High and He not be offended as He is with That Great Babylonian Harlot at Rome, her Harlot Christian Daughters, the Nation of Islam, the Whole of the House of Levi and the Whole of the House of Judah, and the heathen Tribes of the Gentiles. Yea, know all these things, for they are but a portion of the Legacy of Truth and True Righteousness you shall leave the world in all its damnations."

**THE BRIEFINGS PRIOR TO AND
AUDIENCE BEFORE THE MOST HIGH**

171.   Lord El Aku: "Sir!"

172.   Seraphim Ophaniel: "Son of Abraham, Son of Isaac, Son of Ishmael, Son of Jacob, Son of David, El Aku ALIHA ASUR HIGH, Living Anointed Son of The Most High Lord of All Spirits, know that each and every government in the whole world is equally guilty of the same sins, atrocities, iniquities, abuses, abominations, damnations and injustices. Thus they are and thus they are seen in The Sight of The Most High. And they are all equally without excuse in The Sight of The Most High. Know that because all governments, politicians, bureaucrats and all their fellows are abominations in The Sight of The Most High, the Greater Testimony against them is your Testimony and the Testimony of the True and Righteous Akurians. It shall not come to pass that any sins, atrocities, iniquities, abuses, abominations, damnations or injustices of any government, politician, bureaucrat or fellow shall escape the Testimony of the Akurians; and that Testimony, be it against them, shall burn each and every politician and bureaucrat and fellow without exception and without mercy in the Great Depths of Hell. You have no obligation to consider any government, politician, bureaucrat or fellow on their behalf, and each and every government, politician, bureaucrat and fellow has every obligation to consider you on your behalf."

173.   Lord El Aku: "Sir!"

174. Seraphim Zophiel: "Son of Abraham, Son of Isaac, Son of Ishmael, Son of Jacob, Son of David, El Aku ALIHA ASUR HIGH, Living Anointed Son of The Most High Lord of All Spirits, know that each and every religion in the whole world, save the Akurians only, is in knowingly, direct and deliberate violation of the Holy Statutes, their belief notwithstanding. Thus they are and thus they are seen in The Sight of The Most High. And they are all equally without excuse in The Sight of The Most High. All the Holy Statutes are for the benefit of all Creation, and it serves throughout all Creation. Even we of The Great Presence know you and the Akurians adhere only to the Holy Statutes and teach only the Holy Statutes, thus are you hated and despised by all other mankind; nevertheless, your Truth and the Righteousness of The Most High shall prevail. The Most High shall ask you concerning this Generation of Fire and the generations until Shiloh, and He shall speak to the whole world in that same time that all who will hear Him shall hear Him, and all that will not hear Him shall not hear Him justifying His Own Deaf Ear to all they shall present as unto Him. Know that only you and your Akurians have access to, power and authority with The Most High, and nobody else upon the whole earth and nobody else in the whole world. Let them claim what they will; you and the True and Righteous Akurians are living Testimony against them: religions, churches, governments and all the establishments of man."

THE BRIEFINGS PRIOR TO AND AUDIENCE BEFORE THE MOST HIGH

175. Lord El Aku: "Sir!"

176. The Archangels brought forth the Akashic Records, the Book of Life, and revealed again all the details of those who did these damnations knowingly, and knowing the penalties for those violations. And I saw the Earth and all about it that are mine by earned right and Holy Law in accordance with The Will of The Most High. It is my good pleasure, as it has been by all the Anointeds and their Disciples before me, to permit nature to take its own course as established in the beginning of the earth and unchanged, except by man, ever since. It is not my pleasure that the planet be polluted and destroyed that any should profit over any other, whether man or wildlife. There is sufficient in nature, and nature must not be destroyed under any conditions; but the Levites, the Jews, the Christians, the Muslims, the Hindus, the Buddhists, Gentiles and all governments make every effort to profit for now without any consideration for tomorrow's requirements of their own generations. Their combined damnations are uncountable except by The Most High.

177. And I say clearly and without complications to the Elders of the House of Levi and the Elders of the House of Judah who lead this vile parade: Stop all your damnables, selling both sides of every issue that the whole world suffer because you have prevented decision and suppressed truth.

178. And I say clearly and without complications to all Levites, Jews, Marxists, Communists, Fascists,

Catholics, Christians, Muslims, Hindus, Buddhists and Gentiles: Whether you are in religion, government, media or living anywhere in the world, and whether you profess to be a Seeker of Truth, peace or murder: Stop all your damnables, For I will return them upon your own head and upon the heads of all your fellows and upon all your respective generations after you until The Most High stays my Righteous Power and my Holy Authority at Shiloh.

179. Anyone who will may look within their own soul and know Truth from their own innate. Those that do will find all these things, and immeasurably much more, to be truth, irrevocable, and consistently verifiable. Those who do not will find themselves guilty of deliberately ignoring The Most High in the coming Judgments.

180. Anyone with a prudent mind can prove to themselves in very few minutes that each and every disaster anywhere on this planet, except those of nature, fires, floods, earthquakes, volcanic eruptions, et cetera, is the result of some Kak Jew-Socialist Agenda, and even the administration of the after-effects of those are administered into greater harm and hardship on the victims by Kak Jew-Socialists (the United States' Katrina Hurricane being one of the most blatant examples).

181. I was astounded at the number of deceived who think there will be a "rapture" before Hell itself consumes the world. I am appalled at the blatant stupidity of such a damned lie and at the number of those who blindly accept it as absolute truth without

any verification whatsoever. The same fools blindly accept the atrocities of Marx, Engels, Lenin, Stalin, and World Socialism, simply because the lure is so grand sounding. The fact it took Lucifer over 3,000 years to concoct both the damnations of World Socialism and the deceptions of a rapture is beside the point. Everybody who doesn't buy into either one already has the spiritual foundation to escape the ravages of both.

182. The one comfort I found in the Akashic Records going forward in time were the few True and Righteous Akurians who know the Truth and Testify of it at every opportunity, and whose Testimony is absolute in Judgment. That's what Akurians do, they watch, they observe, they see, they hear and they KNOW, that when The Most High asks of them, their Testimony is True; though it send many into the Lake of Eternal Fire and Punishment forever.

183. Seraphim Amatraelonael called the gathering and the Hosts to stand down, ordering the gathering and their Hosts to assemble again, establishing the availability.

AN AKURIAN TRUTH

Have you ever noticed that everything 'the lord puts upon the preacher's heart' is *always taken out of the congregation's ass?*

AKURIAN METAPHYSICAL HANDBOOK
VOLUME I

Scripted from The Akashic Records
THE BRIEFINGS
22 January 2009 – 26 Tevet 5769

184. Seraphim Amatraelonael called the gathering to order and the Hosts to stand easy. I was stationed at the vantage and recognized for the proceedings.

185. Seraphim Amatraelonael: "**Supreme High Priest of All High Priests El Aku ALIHA ASUR HIGH, He That Is Called By The Name of God, the hours are few between this briefing and the Horrors. Indeed, the needless hardships have already begun. Note the perpetration of unspeakable high crimes and treasons against the Whole of the House of Ephraim in the sight of the whole world, and not one investigation, not one indictment, not one trial, not one conviction against the perpetrators who openly steal the wealth and the worth of the Nation and its future.** *None!* **There is no deception. Levites and Jews have stolen and are continuing to steal the entire wealth of the House of Ephraim and are glorified by Levites and Jews who shall subvert any true investigation, and by Levites and Jews who shall suppress all evidence that would require indictment, even though all would be presented to Levites and Jews for trial, who will spare no effort at manipulation toward a "No Bill" from any Grand Jury and a finding of "not guilty" in any court. The Levites and Jews in media again spare no effort to glorify and endorse**

the Marxists Levites and Marxist Jews unto Shiloh, speaking not a word of Righteous Truth."

186.　Lord El Aku: "Sir!"

187.　Seraphim Seraphiel: "Supreme High Priest of All High Priests El Aku ALIHA ASUR HIGH, He That Is Called By The Name of God, there are many Truths upon the earth, seldom heard and even less seldom practiced, and The Irrevocable Curse Of El Aku Upon The Whole Of The House Of Levi and The Irrevocable Curse Of El Aku Upon The Whole Of The House Of Judah is among the most righteous and deserving. In the Years of Tribulation now upon the whole world there shall be scant relief save for those who will know of El Aku's Great Curses and read them. That Tribulation precedes the Horrors and the Horrors precede the Terrors **(destruction, slaughters)** and all precede the Great Intervention is not taught by any of the world's religions, lest they endorse you unto their own detriment and ultimate destruction. When El Aku's Great Curses are presented to all leadership because of its accuracy and True Righteousness, there will be a great wailing from the vile mouths of Levite, Jew, Muslim, Hindu, Buddhist, Catholic and Christian alike; for the Levite and the Jew know they have been irreparably condemned in The Sight of The Most High and all the world, and the Muslims, Hindus, Buddhists, Catholics and Christians shall know they are the Grand Fellows of the Levite's and

Jew's Damnation. They shall all rage against you and all you have written and all who are Proven Knowers of The Great Testimony, sparing nothing to defame, for even the most minor minions of Lucifer know their time is at an end."

188. Lord El Aku: "Sir!"

189. Seraphim Jehoel: "Supreme High Priest of All High Priests El Aku ALIHA ASUR HIGH, He That Is Called By The Name of God, the spirits of the dead are in your hand and must obey your commands to them. Though you interfere not with Righteous Abel's First Judgment, those souls who died unjustly are ever in your debt because of your mercy upon them. Even so, they obey you not because of your mercy but because you are Holy and True and Righteous in The Sight and The Presence of The Most High; and that by earned right. Know that we, The Great Seraphim of The Holy Presence, have presented petition to The Most High on your behalf that you be given Righteous Power and Holy Authority to bestow your earned powers and authorities of the souls of the dead upon all your True and Righteous Akurians. We shall caution the True and Righteous Proven Knowers of The Great Testimony concerning Righteous Abel's First Judgment, that they interfere not nor mollify it in any manner. This we have done in the Days of your Protocols and now the Days of the Risen Dead are come, to our great satisfaction. Those who will rise at Lord

Horseman Immanuel's beckon will rejoice with us even as the Days of Holocaust and the Years of Tribulation consume the unrighteous. Those who mock and despise you and the Proven Knowers now will scream your name the loudest that you hear their supplication and bring them relief and salvation from the damnations they are bringing down upon their own heads and the heads of their generations after them, Yea, and at their own hands. And the True and Righteous Akurians and the Risen Dead shall testify against them."

190.   Lord El Aku: "Sir!"

191.   Seraphim Kemuel: "Supreme High Priest of All High Priests El Aku ALIHA ASUR HIGH, He That Is Called By The Name of God, You who are taught directly out of The Glorious Mouth of The Most High: The Great Audience is near and on schedule, Lucifer and all his Officers and minions are rampant to destroy all that cannot be left behind of the Whole of the House of Ephraim, the Whole of the House of Manasseh, and the whole world. In a civilization of husbandry, it is only necessary to burn the fields prior to harvest to weaken that civilization unto quick destruction. In a civilization of industry, it is only necessary to burn the accesses of delivery to weaken that civilization unto quick destruction. In a civilization of commerce, it is only necessary to burn the currency to weaken that civilization unto quick destruction. And in all the House of Joseph, even Israel, there is

no smoke of burning of the currency for the Whole of the House of Levi and the Whole of the House of Judah and their Marxist collaborators have stolen the entire wealth of Ephraim and the entire wealth of Manasseh in the light of day when they who did the stealing were on watch against thieves and bandits. Thus they are and thus they are seen in The Sight of The Most High. The whole of the House of Levi have become a vile abomination, and the Whole of the House of Judah have become a putrid damnation in The Sight of The Most High; and neither possess any access to or righteousness before The Most High, nor any access to or righteousness before any who are True and Righteous before The Most High, even we Seraphim of The Holy Presence. Therefore, their repentance must be unto you, as you shall require it, and as you shall require of them. As you shall declare it to be unto Shiloh, so shall it be unto Shiloh."

192. Lord El Aku: "Sir!"

193. Seraphim Nethanael: "Supreme High Priest of All High Priests El Aku ALIHA ASUR HIGH, He That Is Called By The Name of God, You who have direct access to The Most High, who hears in His Own Ear all things in all Creation: The cries of the oppressed and the abandoned of the whole world are rampant, and many, and loud and long. The Most High is sore offended at the Whole of the House of Joseph in their toleration and surrender to all things knowingly evil, and direct violat-

ion of the Holy Statutes, and their toleration and surrender to all things knowingly vile and evil of the Whole of the House of Levi and the Whole of the House of Judah until all the vile and evil are the law of the land in the Whole of the House of Joseph. And now the Whole of the House of Joseph stand in their own gates and watch as the Whole of the House of Levi and the Whole of the House of Judah carry off even the minds and souls of the children along with all the other wealth. The whole of the House of Joseph whine and moan of the grief and disaster and plague upon them, and none of the Whole of the House of Joseph shall dare to speak to identify any Levite or any Jew or any Marxist lest they be reviled, arrested and incarcerated in their nonexistent freedoms. Yea, the Levite and the Jew and the Marxist have stolen even the liberty to think and to reason, lest a prudent mind reveal the truth and the Levite and the Jew and the Marxist be taken outside the gate and stoned to death for their abominations in accordance with the Holy Statutes. This you have inherited and this you will destroy, even at the expense of the whole world that such evil be put out from and be no more found in all Creation."

194. Lord El Aku: "Sir!"

195. Seraphim Ophaniel: "Supreme High Priest of All High Priests El Aku ALIHA ASUR HIGH, He That Is Called By The Name of God, Holy and Righteous Son of the Righteous Fire of Abraham,

the Whole of the House of Levi and the Whole of the House of Judah have made themselves the most vile of all abominations in The Sight of The Most High. Thus they are and thus they are seen in The Sight of The Most High. The Most High has sent His Attending Angels to the Whole of the House of Levi and to the Whole of the House of Judah, into every household, into every market place, into every office, into every shop, into every lodge, onto every highway and into every Synagogue to see and hear of them each and every one, and to report to Him of that which they did and that which they did not encounter, that He would know without exception the truth of Levi and Judah. The Attending Angels went forth and observed each and every living entity of the Levites and each every living entity of Judah. The Attending Angels found none worthy before The Most High; none worthy of truth; none worthy of righteousness; and none worthy of your consideration save to Testify against them. We have witnessed your Testimony before The Most High against the Whole of the House of Levi, the Whole of the House of Judah, the Whole of the House of Joseph and the Whole of the Tribes of Jacob and the Whole of the Children of Abraham and of Ishmael; and we witness that your Testimony before The Most High was true in the hour of your presentation, and your Testimony before The Most High is true in The Sight of The Most High as you now prepare for The Great Audience."

**THE BRIEFINGS PRIOR TO AND
AUDIENCE BEFORE THE MOST HIGH**

196. Lord El Aku: "Sir!"

197. Seraphim Zophiel: "Supreme High Priest of All High Priests El Aku ALIHA ASUR HIGH, He That Is Called By The Name of God, Holy and Righteous Son of the Righteous Fire of Ishmael and Israel, the Fires of Hell you are about to bring down upon the whole world in this Hour of Justification are but a pittance of the Great Fury of The Wrath of The Most High yet to come. Know that all the abominations must cease or there will be no flesh left alive anywhere upon the whole earth. When you deprive the whole world of peace, relief, security and comfort, there are none alive or who will live during the times of your Great Curses that will fully comprehend the extent of the agonies you and the Akurians shall inflict in Righteous Indignation. Your pronouncements upon the whole world shall be so severe that even the Marxists, Communists, Fascists, Catholics, Christians, Muslims, Hindus, Buddhists, Gentiles, Atheists, Levites and Jews shall scream amighty unto The Most High, who will not hear them. They will bellow your name more than they denounce it this day for you to save them from their own damnations, and you will not hear them either. And the worst is yet to come: The Great Fury of The Wrath of The Most High. Even your beloved Akurians will know these hardships and the source of them; but they shall rejoice that Justice is finally accomplished upon the vile and the evil, and upon the Whole of the House of

Joseph for its tolerance of the abominations of the Marxists, Communists, Fascists, Catholics, Christians, Muslims, Hindus, Buddhists, Gentiles, Atheists, Levites and Jews at the instigation and enforcement of the Whole of the House of Levi and the Whole of the House of Judah with their powers of office. Behold, the Marxists, Communists, Fascists, Catholics, Christians, Muslims, Hindus, Buddhists, Gentiles, Atheists, Levites and Jews have all defiled The Holy Name, even The Name Named Upon You by The Most High, Himself – ALIHA ASUR HIGH – His Own True and Holy Name. Therefore, in the Hour of Justification: spare them not!"

198. Lord El Aku: "Sir!"

199. The Archangels brought forth the Akashic Records, the Book of Life, and revealed again all the details of those who did these damnations knowingly, and knowing the penalties for those violations.

200. In reviewing all these things in the Akashic Records, I came to the conclusion that in the days to come when those who will become Righteous want to know these same things in infinite detail, there should be a marker of where I looked and what I saw of everything recorded there. The Most High put a Marker of Light showing the beginning and ending of what I saw and where I went next in the exact sequence. It's a simple ring at the starting point of a segment, showing the location of the

segment I viewed before, and continuing as a bright tube until I finished with that segment, the ending ring showing where I went to next. Really very simple to describe, a section marked out with a brighter light background and rings on each end showing where I was before and where I went to next. Actually, it is an indescribable miracle by The Most High that cannot be duplicated by anyone else, as it does not interfere with any of the Akashic Records in their original design or their absolute accuracy.

201. That I saw Nefilim and other extraterrestrials alongside Demons in their damnations and Angels in their resistance to them, is a matter well recorded there for all to see. The damned lies of a totally nonexistent 'rapture' and 'Jesus coming **before** all these things' are shown in all their filth and deception. Designed to deceive and entrap millions, they have done their work well. If you have any doubts, ask the nearest hallelujah halfwit. They are still in over their heads in both stupidities.

202. All the accolades of me by the Great Seraphim and everything spoken by The Most High during His Direct Intervention are scant comfort to me as I know the horrors I must call down on a spiritually and morally bereft generation of harlotmongers, harlots, racemixers, child abusers, murderers, traitors, liars, thieves and conspirators. Were they not mingled among those too damnably stupid to recognize them for what they really are, and those too damnably cowardly to call them into proper account, I would send their destruction without

hesitation. But because they are mingled with the damnably stupid and cowardly, as well as the truly innocent, the destructions will be flush with collateral damage never seen before in the history of mankind. Even so, I will not spare the fire nor the brimstone nor even the precious honey bee nor the budding flower. The whole world will rue the day they brought The Most High to this Fury; and the Whole of the House of Levi and the Whole of the House of Judah will receive the worst of it; even as the Whole of the House of Canaan and the Whole of the House of Cush receive their due first. I am a Warrior by Creation and I am about to receive my marching orders.

203. Seraphim Amatraelonael called the gathering and the Hosts to stand down, ordering the gathering and their Hosts to assemble again, establishing the availability.

MOTION PICTURES, PHONORECORDS AND MUSIC PUBLISHING GROUP

The Holy Order's Entertainment Company, still licensing all fields of music World Wide. Referred to below in The Holy Presence during Testimony before The Most High against Kak Jews and Levite Priest Sons of Aaron.

**THE BRIEFINGS PRIOR TO AND
AUDIENCE BEFORE THE MOST HIGH**

Scripted from The Akashic Records
THE BRIEFINGS
23 January 2009 – 27 Tevet 5769

204. Seraphim Amatraelonael called the gathering to order and the Hosts to stand easy. I was stationed at the vantage and recognized for the proceedings.

205. Seraphim Amatraelonael: "Supreme Lord of All Supreme Lords El Aku ALIHA ASUR HIGH, Upon Whom The Most High has Named His Own Name, Warrior of Warriors, the whole world has preferred war at the instigation of the Whole of the House of Levi and the Whole of the House of Judah and the Whole of the House of Ishmael and many Houses of the Gentiles, therefore, spare them not! Among the Tribulations you shall Pronounce in your Hour of Justification: Deliver war upon every doorstep and upon every blade of grass and into every drop of rain and flake of snow. Spare not anyone nor anything, lest you leave an encampment of enemies behind you to the detriment of the Beloved Akurians. Deliver war into the farthest corners and unto the darkest reaches and leave only war unquenched in your wake. And in those Days of the Tribulation of War when every Levite and every Jew shall whine another layer of Disguised Damnations of Marxism and Abominations of Socialism seeking more for themselves and less for all others, they shall be stoned in the streets as a sacrifice to appease the

Gods of War that there might be a moment of peace in that time."

206. Lord El Aku: "Sir!"

207. Seraphim Seraphiel: "Supreme Lord of All Supreme Lords El Aku ALIHA ASUR HIGH, Upon Whom The Most High has Named His Own Name, Warrior of Warriors, the whole world has preferred their own enslavement at the instigation of the Whole of the House of Levi and the Whole of the House of Judah and the Whole of the House of Ishmael and many Houses of the Gentiles; therefore, spare them not! Among the Tribulations you shall Pronounce in your Hour of Justification: Deliver their own enslavement without mercy and without consideration, even upon the truly innocent. Whether slavery come by force of arms or force of law, slavery is slavery, and this enslavement shall not be as slavery by temporary bondage whereof the enslaved has both security and protection, but by merciless Levites, Jews, Marxists, Communists, Fascists and Demonic Socialists as shall be the most acceptable of the people. Deliver bondage unspeakable upon every house and upon every housetop that none escape either the eye or the rage of the enslaver. Remove pity from all your considerations, for neither the Levite, nor the Jew, nor the Ishmaelite, nor the Gentile, shall consider pity even unto blood of their own blood and bone of their own bones in their days of power. Spare them not, until even the uppermost

slave master cannot escape the agonies and miseries and hopelessness as suffered by the lowest slave in the lowest and dirtiest sewer. When infested sackcloth shall be the most glorious of raiment and dung the most exquisite meal and a cesspool the most comfortable castle, then shall all those who know of the Akurians say, "Blessed are those who come in the True Name of The Most High," and in those Days of the Tribulation of total enslavement when every Levite and every Jew shall whine another layer of Disguised Damnations of Marxism and Abominations of Socialism seeking more for themselves and less for all others, they shall be stoned in the streets as a sacrifice to appease the Gods of Enslavement that there might be a moment of relief in that time."

208. Lord El Aku: "Sir!"

209. Seraphim Jehoel: "Supreme Lord of All Supreme Lords El Aku ALIHA ASUR HIGH, Upon Whom The Most High has Named His Own Name, Warrior of Warriors, the whole world has preferred economic recession and economic depression at the instigation of the Whole of the House of Levi and the Whole of the House of Judah and the Whole of the House of Ishmael and many Houses of the Gentiles; therefore, spare them not! Among the Tribulations you shall Pronounce in your Hour of Justification: Deliver economic recession and economic depression that the whole worth of the Whole of the Nation be less than a farthing, and

the Whole of the House of Levi and the Whole of the House of Judah and the Whole of the House of Ishmael and the many Houses of the Gentiles shall have ought of it. Nothing. That the Whole of the House of Levi and the Whole of the House of Judah and the Whole of all their fellows be separated from all their own honest wealth and separated from all the wealth they have stolen from all others; that they have not a pence to present before The Most High. Did not the Righteous Daughters of Akuria, even the Righteous Daughters of Elisha, require before The Most High that all Levites and all Jews and all their fellows be deprived of all their worth and value, both earned and stolen? Yea, we were all in The Great Presence in that hour, and we are all Direct Witnesses that The Most High did hear them and did approve their petition. And in those Days of the Tribulation of economic recession and economic depression when every Levite and every Jew shall whine another layer of Disguised Damnations of Marxism and Abominations of Socialism seeking more for themselves and less for all others, they shall be stoned in the streets as a sacrifice to appease the Gods of Gold and Finance that there might be a moment of sustenance in that time."

210. Lord El Aku: "Sir!"

211. Seraphim Kemuel: "Supreme Lord of All Supreme Lords El Aku ALIHA ASUR HIGH, Upon Whom The Most High has Named His Own Name,

THE BRIEFINGS PRIOR TO AND AUDIENCE BEFORE THE MOST HIGH

Warrior of Warriors, the whole world has preferred epidemic crime at the instigation of the Whole of the House of Levi and the Whole of the House of Judah and the Whole of the House of Ishmael and many Houses of the Gentiles; therefore, spare them not! Among the Tribulations you shall Pronounce in your Hour of Justification: Deliver epidemic crime upon every Socialist, upon every publican, upon every high office, upon every officer, upon every prosecutor, upon every lawyer, upon every accountant, upon every judge, upon every criminal, upon every head, upon every house, upon every market, upon every street, upon every highway, upon every coward, upon every Levite, upon every Jew, upon every Synagogue, upon every Lodge, upon every Catholic, upon every Christian, upon every church, upon every Muslim, upon every mosque, upon every Hindu, upon every Temple, upon every Buddhist, upon every Shrine, upon every Mausoleum, upon every graveyard, upon all who insist the citizen be disarmed and defenseless in the face of danger until all scream for unfettered and uninfringed possession of slaying weapons in their own defense. And in those Days of the Tribulation of epidemic crime when every Levite and every Jew shall whine another layer of Disguised Damnations of Marxism and Abominations of Socialism seeking more for themselves and less for all others, they shall be stoned in the streets as a sacrifice to appease the Gods of Epidemic Crime that there might be a moment of safety in that time."

212. Lord El Aku: "Sir!"

213. Seraphim Nethanael: "Supreme Lord of All Supreme Lords El Aku ALIHA ASUR HIGH, Upon Whom The Most High has Named His Own Name, Warrior of Warriors, the whole world has preferred ethnic cleansing and merciless death at the instigation of the Whole of the House of Levi and the Whole of the House of Judah and the Whole of the House of Ishmael and many Houses of the Gentiles; therefore, spare them not! Among the Tribulations you shall Pronounce in your Hour of Justification: Deliver ethnic cleansing and merciless death upon every family, upon every Tribe, upon every People and upon every Nation until the bloodshed and slaughter shall be as prevalent in the bedchamber of the new bride and new groom as it shall be in the battlezones of great engagements. Deliver ethnic cleansing and merciless death so rampant there shall be not a blade of grass nor a court of law that is not spattered with the blood of the slain. Deliver ethnic cleansing and merciless death so rampant there shall be neither hymn nor prayer at the disposal of the corpse. Deliver ethnic cleansing and merciless death so rampant the vultures shall dance because there is no more hunger among them, and they shall not make preparation for long fasts. Deliver ethnic cleansing and merciless death so rampant that even the dung eaters shall be filled and their stomachs satisfied. And in those Days of the Tribulation of ethnic cleansing and merciless

death when every Levite and every Jew shall whine another layer of Disguised Damnations of Marxism and Abominations of Socialism seeking more for themselves and less for all others, they shall be stoned in the streets as a sacrifice to appease the Gods of Ethnic Cleansing and Merciless Death that there might be a moment of life the Angels of Death do not deplore in that time."

214.   Lord El Aku: "Sir!"

215.   Seraphim Ophaniel: "Supreme Lord of All Supreme Lords El Aku ALIHA ASUR HIGH, Upon Whom The Most High has Named His Own Name, Warrior of Warriors, the whole world has preferred plagues inflicted by governments at the instigation of the Whole of the House of Levi and the Whole of the House of Judah and the Whole of the House of Ishmael and many Houses of the Gentiles; therefore, spare them not! Among the Tribulations you shall Pronounce in your Hour of Justification: Deliver plagues inflicted by governments in uncountable numbers and incurable severity. How knows the governments a season and a year in advance the coming epidemic? How knows the governments a season and a year in advance that they prepare at great expense to the people and great profit to the pharmaceuticals which medication? Are there True Prophets ministering in governments, the dominion and domain of all manner of Demons and infinite evil? Nay, True Prophets are the enemies of governments, of

Demons, and infinite evil. There are only murderers and liars about murderers in the halls of governments dominated by Levites and Jews and their Marxist Legislations and Demons of high and low stature, all practitioners of infinite evil. Thus they are and thus they are seen in The Sight of The Most High. And thus is your Testimony against them. And in those Days of the Tribulation of Plagues when every Levite and every Jew shall whine another layer of Disguised Damnations of Marxism and Abominations of Socialism seeking more for themselves and less for all others, they shall be stoned in the streets as a sacrifice to appease the Gods of Endless Plagues that there might be a moment of healing in that time."

216. Lord El Aku: "Sir!"

217. Seraphim Zophiel: "Supreme Lord of All Supreme Lords El Aku ALIHA ASUR HIGH, Upon Whom The Most High has Named His Own Name, Warrior of Warriors, the whole world has preferred famine at the instigation of the Whole of the House of Levi and the Whole of the House of Judah and the Whole of the House of Ishmael and many Houses of the Gentiles; therefore, spare them not! Among the Tribulations you shall Pronounce in your Hour of Justification: Deliver famine everywhere growth shall attempt to take root; deliver famine so severe the farmer shall see more increase from fences than from gardens; deliver famine so severe the rich and opulent shall

beg in the streets and search the sewers for dung; deliver famine so severe that only the scavengers of the wild shall not know hunger; deliver famine so severe that mere emaciation shall appear a thing of beauty. And in those Days of the Tribulation of Great Famine when every Levite and every Jew shall whine another layer of Disguised Damnations of Marxism and Abominations of Socialism seeking more for themselves and less for all others, they shall be stoned in the streets as a sacrifice to appease the Gods of Great Famine that there might be a morsel of sustenance in that time. And there shall be no relief until the whole world has learned its lessons, and the Holy Statutes are the Law of all the lands, and every knee shall bow and every tongue shall confess, "Blessed are the True Akurians, for they testified against us and brought down the Great Wrath of The Most High. Blessed be The Name of The Most High, ALIHA ASUR HIGH, in all the Heavens and in all the Earths."

218. Lord El Aku: "Sir!"

219. The Archangels brought forth the Akashic Records, the Book of Life, and revealed again all the details of those who did these damnations knowingly, and knowing the penalties for those violations. Of all the abominations, treasons, treacheries, collusions and conspiracies recorded of mankind in the Akashic Records, there were no greater perpetrators than the House of Levi and the House of Judah and That Great Babylonian Harlot at Rome.

The atrocities of the Christians and the Nation of Islam combined do not compare. The greater atrocities began with the creation of Socialism by the Levite and Jew funded Karl Marx and Friedrich Engels. The spread of Socialism began a bloodshed of innocents greater than all the wars and religious conversion campaigns, and continues to this very day. There is no greater practice of Demonism than Socialism, whether Communist or Fascist, as both are from the same source: Levi, Judah and That Great Babylonian Harlot at Rome. Now it has infested and infected the entire Nation of Islam and every sovereign Nation on earth.

220. The only process for the Final Solution for Peace on Earth is the total extermination of all Marxists, Communists, Fascists, Socialists and Progressives of whatsoever stripe. Spare them and they will destroy you. They will destroy you in your own home, in your own streets, in your neighborhood, in your schools, in your place of worship, in your generations after you, in your place of employment, in your entertainment, in your banking, in your purchases, in your marketing and in your sales, as they already have in your governments and in your access to news and information. Their destructions are never ending; they have infested and infected each and every nook and cranny of civilization and always to the detriment of all others concerned.

221. And the worst is yet to come.

THE BRIEFINGS PRIOR TO AND AUDIENCE BEFORE THE MOST HIGH

THE AUDIENCE
3 February 2009 – 9 Sh'vat 5769

222. I spent the entire interim from 24 January 2009 – 28 Tevet 5769 until 30 January 2009 – 5 Sh'vat 5769 in preparation and rehearsal of the many facts and points of truth given during the briefing. I went over things I am a Master at in the Heavens. I must be absolute in everything I am going to do to the damnables of this world and those in their company. I must set given points that when a given iniquity is full, it will trigger additional points of The Most High's Great Wrath by due Justification. I must make sure all the deceptions are uncovered, that the testimony against those who will do nothing against the perpetrators will bring additional Hell down on both their own heads as they fully deserve. I do not take these things lightly, as the world is about to learn the hard way.

223. Having prepared myself and dressed in full armor, and in the Company of Lord Horseman Immanuel and His Command, Lord Horseman Horus and His Command and Lord Horseman Hammerlin and His Command, I presented myself and My Command to the Great Seraphim of The Holy Presence. Full formalities and recognitions required. Upon the Great Area before the Great Veil of The Most High, the Honored and the Righteous entered in a Pass in Review that I should know the muster of the gathering. Each of the Great Seraphim, *except* Lucifer, who is forbidden access to The Holy Presence until and unless directly sum-

moned; Urakabarameel, who I killed in The Holy Presence at the Great Fall; and Aeshmodeva, The Raging Fiend, who I killed November 27th, 1976 **(GCAD)** – 6 Kislev 5737 **(Hebrew)**.

224. All the Commanding Angels of the Orders of Angels from the highest to the lowest were in presence in accordance with their rank and station, including the Seven Great Archangels and their Commands. The Hosts of Heaven stood in honor beyond my ability to number, command by command, unit by unit, rank by rank, station by station, upward and outward as far as I cared to see. The True Saints and the Anointed Messiahs of their Generations and most of their Disciples were in presence, as were the Patriarchs of the Children of Abraham. This many in number, of these ranks and stations should indicate to the prudent mind the degree of importance to the remaining generations, be it few or many, until Shiloh. That it will offend all the priests, preachers and other liars along with their hallelujah halfwit followers, because they were *not* there and I was, is as sure and certain as it is beside the point.

225. We presented ourselves before The Great Veil in accordance with our rank and station in accordance with our respective assignment. Once presented, I was called forth to the Place of Recognition, escorted by the other Three Great Horsemen and our Commands. First Great Horseman Immanuel and His Command on my left, Third Great Horseman Horus and His Command and Fourth Great

THE BRIEFINGS PRIOR TO AND AUDIENCE BEFORE THE MOST HIGH

Horseman Hammerlin and His Command in that order on my right.

226. I saluted for all of us, "**Most High Lord of Hosts, the Great Horsemen of Your Command are present and accounted in proper muster.**"

227. And The Most High spoke, ""**Son of Fire, Son of Fire, Beloved Son of My Service, concerning the Hour of Justification of the whole world: That those who will hear may hear; and those who will be of My Holy Law in all Righteousness will be recognized; and those who will continue their abominations in My Sight will be abandoned to be trampled into their own sewers of suffering under their own feet.**

228. ""**Hear Me, oh, Earth, for your ears are not ears of stone.**

229. ""**Hear Me, oh, Generations of Ish, for your ears hear and listen not.**

230. ""**Hear Me, oh, Generations of Abraham, for your ears and eyes have long been closed unto Me.**

231. ""**Hear Me, oh, Generations of Ishmael, for your ears and eyes see Justice only in a sword.**

232. ""**Hear Me, oh, Generations of Isaac, for your ears and eyes are as the deaf and the blind.**

233. ""**Hear Me, oh, Generations of Jacob, for your ears and eyes are as doors shut against all Creation.**

234. ""**Hear Me, oh, Generation of Fire, for your ears shall hear the Great Thunder of My Fury, and your eyes shall see the beginning of My Great Wrath unto Shiloh.**

235. ""Hear Me, all who will stand before Me and give full account, for your very existence rests upon your own head and within your own hand; therefore, let not your ears deceive you with grand lies of Socialism nor your eyes deceive you with grand displays of that Babylonian Harlot at Rome nor the wiles of any of her Harlot Christian Daughters.

236. ""Hear Me, all who claim My Righteousness and have it not: for only My Beloved Akurians practice My Righteousness, and of My Beloved Akurians only is My Testimony. Let not your Abominations of Damnation come near the hearing nor the sight nor the presence of any of My Beloved Akurians, lest it be an Eternal Testimony against you upon your own head and at your own hand.

237. ""Hear Me, oh, Levi; Hear Me, oh, Judah: your Abominations of Damnation are neither hidden from My Sight nor secret from your intended victims. And I will not abide your desecrations of the Whole of the Birthright House of Joseph, even Ephraim and Manasseh, nor the Whole of the Houses of Israel, nor the Whole of the Houses of Ishmael, nor the Whole of the Tribes of all the Gentiles. For in the Day your instigations shall bring unrighteous fire **(nuclear war, chemical, germ warfare)** upon any innocent seed I will include you and all yours and all your fellows and all your respective generations after you in the hail, even upon the whole world unto Shiloh.

238.   ""Hear Me, oh, Generations of Ishmael, for I see your destructions of the innocent and your Abominations of Damnation to expand My Righteousness with violence and with death. And I will not abide your desecrations of the Whole of the Birthright House of Joseph, even Ephraim and Manasseh, nor the Whole of the Houses of Israel, nor the Whole of the Houses of Ishmael, nor the Whole of the Tribes of all the Gentiles. For in the Day your instigations shall bring unrighteous death **(nuclear war, chemical, germ warfare)** upon any innocent seed I will include you and all yours and all your fellows and all your respective generations after you in the hail, even upon the whole world unto Shiloh.

239.   ""Hear Me, oh, Generation of Fire, lest you become the First Generation of the Damned!

240.   ""Son of Fire, Son of Fire, Beloved Son of My Service, this is the Hour of Justification of the whole world. Are you prepared to proceed?""

241.   I answered, "Sir!"

242.   ""Son of Fire, My Own Anointed in the Earth, I know your good service unto Me, and I know all the Abominations and Damnations done against you because you are a good service unto Me. Therefore, the iniquity of the Whole of the House of the Tribes of Ishmael, the Whole of the House of the Tribes of Israel, specifically the Whole of the House of Levi and the Whole of the House of Judah, and the Whole of the

congregations of That Great Babylonian Harlot at Rome and the Whole of all her Harlot Christian Daughters is full as of the Full Moon, 16 Sh'vat 5769 **(9 February 2009 GCAD).**""

243. I answered, "Sir!"

244. ""Son of Fire, My Holy Prince of War, I know your Testimonies Against the Abominations of Damnation of My Children of Abraham, That Great Babylonian Harlot at Rome and her Harlot Christian Daughters. By the Righteous Powers and Holy Authorities of your Holy Office in My Name upon the whole Earth, say now the hour of the Beginning of the Hour of Justification upon the whole world.""

245. I answered, "Sir, the 1st Day of Adar 1, 5769, being the 25th Day of February, 2009 **(GCAD)**, in the first hour as the moon goes new.
246. "Sir, I direct that any part of these invocations in This Audience before You be part of all other invocations in This Audience before You. I and the Akurians shall increase and refine the invocations as we deem appropriate."

247. ""It is done.
248. ""Son of Fire, My Holy Avenger in the Earth, the Whole of the Children of Abraham have polluted many of themselves and their generations with Accursed Canaan knowing My Absolute prohibition of such abomination, written clearly in

My Holy Statutes. Thus they are and thus is your Testimony against them, and thus they are seen in My Sight. And thus they are condemned.

249. ""See you across the way My Servant Abraham, even though an Honored Man of My Own Presence, he is sore ashamed of such Blasphemy Against the Holy Spirit of Truth by any of his children and the many abominations against justice committed in My Name. From the Hour of Justification unto Shiloh, I will not have pity, neither will Mine Eye spare, for I have been Blasphemed; My Name is a laughingstock in the mouth of the Whole of the Children of Abraham; My Holy Statutes are naught in the courts of the land; and My Holy Ones are persecuted as common criminals.

250. ""Son of Fire, Son of Fire, from the Hour of Justification there shall be no more mercy upon the whole world because of Accursed Canaan and the harlotmongering of the Children of Abraham.

251. ""Say you more against them?""

252. I answered, "Sir, that it is clear: I will not spare any Socialist or Socialist Agenda; any false religion including Judaism and Islam, for they have both betrayed the Righteousness; and the Doctrines of Death of That Great Babylonian Harlot at Rome including all her Harlot Christian Daughters; any court of any law that is in any violation of the Constitution of the United States; nor any Abomination against Holy Law.

253. "Sir, being a victim without Holy Appointment and being a victim with Holy Appointment, I say also against the Lodges, against the Institutions, against the Governments and all the Courts of the Land, and against the Religions. By my Great Sword am I against them, and against them all; and I shall send the sins of them all upon all their generations after them until Shiloh. There shall be no peace anywhere among them, and their greatest enemies shall be their nearest family and their nearest fellow. The more they struggle to stand in their Abominations of Damnation, the more they shall falter and the more they shall fall. All their efforts shall gain them nothing except their own Damnations upon their own heads at their own hands.

254. "Sir, to Accursed Canaan and Accursed Cush I have sent the transcripts of the Great Curses upon them that they know their own errors and return to Holy Law, knowing that only total adherence to Holy Law will bring them deliverance in their generations. That I have done this has raised a great deal of anger toward me and my Holy Office, most of it from Accursed Canaan and Accursed Cush and those who advocate and practice racemixing and the Blasphemy Against the Holy Spirit of Truth. There shall be no peace anywhere and violence shall expand everywhere among Accursed Canaan and be rife upon all the Blasphemers, leaving death upon every doorstep and in every house and in every street and byway. But I will show deserved compassion to all of

Cush who will return to Holy Law and come out of Canaan before That Great and Dreadful Day.

255. "Sir, to all who will be Righteous, I command to be Righteous now, for I will not spare you tomorrow or forever. To all who will serve The True and Living God, ALIHA ASUR HIGH, I command to declare so now and be about that business, for if I cannot call upon you in this hour, I will not call upon you at all. To all who will incur my anger, you shall have it in full measure in the world now and in Hell Eternal. To this Great Company gathered in this Holy Place: Bear me witness that I will not spare the unrepentant nor delay my own removal of peace from the earth upon all the generations in this hour nor all the generations until Shiloh.

256. "Sir, even so, I will not knowingly harm any True Righteous."

257. ""It is done.

258. ""Spare not any in the Company of the Damned! If they are True Righteous I will make full recompense; and I will not stay your hand.

259. ""Son of Fire, Son of My Righteous Indignation, know that when I send the Hosts of My Wrath upon the whole world, I will slay all the impure blood not of the true blood of the lineage of their fathers whether of Ish, Abraham or of the Gentiles. Pure I made them in the Beginning and Pure I require them now and forever. I will not have My Holy Statutes disobeyed or ignored. Those who are not righteous before you are not

righteous before Me; and in the Days before Shiloh those who are not righteous before the Akurians shall not be righteous before Me. And whosoever is not Righteous is Damned.

260. ""Son of Fire, Holy Son of Abraham, Ishmael, Isaac and Jacob, I have seen the Abominations, even all the Abominations of the Sons of Aaron and Levi; and I am offended in them all as I am offended in their fathers; for they betrayed the Righteousness and sold it in the streets for a farthing as the price of an aged whore for worth and value. And in My Wrath I removed the Ark of My Testimony from them at Jerusalem, vowing upon My Own Self that it shall not return until every Son of Aaron stand sanctified in the Presence of My Holy Anointed One. Lo! The Sons of Aaron have not repented, neither have they delivered any good thing to any of My Anointeds in their generations, and have become more the harlot than Israel in the Days of Isaiah, and more the harlot than Judah in the Days of Nebuchadnezzar. Lo! The whole of the House of Levi is a Harlot in My Sight, mingled with the House of Judah and more unclean than the Children of Cush. Yea, Levi and Judah, Judah and Levi, have chosen to prevail a few hours with Lucifer and abandoned My Eternal Promise, and I will not excuse, neither will I stay My Rod of Iron when I chasten them from the Hour of Justifications until Shiloh.

261. ""Son of Fire, Holy and Righteous Seed of Abraham, I know the Abominations of Damnation

done at the hands of the Whole of the House of Levi and the Whole of the House of Judah upon the Whole of the House of Joseph, even Ephraim and Manasseh, and the Whole of the rest of the world. Yea, I know their conspiracies, their collusions, their grand schemes, their treasons and their treacheries, and I know all their thieveries from the innocent and from the helpless, from all the Tribes and all the Peoples and all the Nations of the world. Yea, I know their conspiracies, collusions, grand schemes, treasons, treacheries and thieveries from generations to come; and I will not spare them nor their own generations from the Hour of Justification unto Shiloh.

262.   ""Son of Fire, Son of Fire, from the Hour of Justification there shall be no more mercy upon the whole world because of the Abominations of Damnation by the Sons of Aaron, the Whole of the Tribe of Levi and the Whole of the Tribe of Judah against the Children of Abraham and the whole world.

263.   ""Say you more against them?""

264.   I answered, "Sir, I have a great deal against many of them, some for decades, some very recent and some a combination of both in their damnable collusions and conspiracies. (In 1959 GCAD Bobby Farrell founded, and the Akurians still operate, Vandor Motion Pictures, Phonorecords and Music Publishing Group.) From the 1940s (GCAD) I have been robbed and ridiculed by the Levites and Jews at ASCAP (American Society of Composers,

Authors and Publishers), BMI (Broadcast Music, Incorporated) and Entertainment and Trade Industry publications wherever and as often as they could do me deliberate harm. While they would spare no effort to omit everything possible of my accomplishments from the industry publications, whether good reports of successes, news releases, articles or advertisements, they also spared no effort to defamate me personally and my investment endeavors at every opportunity; nor have they spared any effort against any of my associates and clientele. But the Kak Jews, which include many Levites, at ASCAP, BMI, SESAC, RIAA (Recording Industry Association of America) and other such self-appointed 'authorities' are not alone. The Lodges, Governments and Major Media have done no less in their efforts to defame, deprive and suppress.

265. "Sir, the current economic extortion and blackmail being perpetrated as I stand in this Holy Presence is being accomplished almost entirely by Kak Jews and Kak Jew-Puppets, many on government payroll committing economic espionage that is clear and present High Treason in direct and deliberate violation of their Oath of Office to protect and defend that Holy Document, the Constitution of the United States, against all enemies foreign and domestic. Those filthy, lying, thieving, murdering bastards are domestic enemies by infiltration, infestation and infection of the Whole of the House of Joseph, Ephraim and Manasseh, and shall be dealt with as such. I am

minded to say of my own as my Colleague, Prophet Zechariah, the son of Berechia, the son of Iddo the Prophet said of You: **(Zechariah 14:21)** "" *... in That Day there shall be no more the Canaanite in the House of The Lord of Hosts;*"" 'in That Day there shall be no more the Kak Jew, whether Jew or Levite **(respecting also the Sons of Aaron)**, in the House of Akuria.' They are a vile and an abominable people, and I am not going to spare them, even until Shiloh.

266. "Sir, the Greatest of All Abominations of Damnation to date is Socialism in all its many facets. Any grain of Socialism almost instantly grows into its own impassable mountain of great-sounding idiocies requiring immeasurable input of more than can ever exist while producing an equally impassable canyon of inexcusable failures. And all Socialism brought upon the earth was and still is by deliberate design of the House of Levi and the House of Judah in collusion with That Great Babylonian Harlot at Rome and all her equally Demonic fallout 'Christian' daughters. Socialism, like Levites and Jews, can never be satisfied because they can never consume enough of other people's money and substance. Any pretense of approval of Socialism, regardless of how small, should be infinite justification for the perpetrator to be taken to the gates and stoned to death in the sight of the people, to put and keep such damnation out of the land and off the entire planet. Were the Levites and the Jews both exterminated in the next hour, the planet would know a

great sweetness in the air and a relief from Socialist Damnations before the clock could sound the time. I will not spare the bastards at any time, for any reason, between my Hour of Justification and Shiloh. What I bring upon them is that which they seek to bring upon the whole world; and none of them shall escape.

267. "Sir, knowing that none dare speak a lie in Your Presence, in Your Holy Presence and in the hearing of this entire gathering: I declare the Demons of Socialism are the Whole of the House of Levi and the Whole of the House of Judah and the Whole of That Great Babylonian Harlot at Rome and all her Harlot Christian Daughters. The Children of Ishmael and their followers among the Gentiles are duped by Beelzebub and will not cast him out from among themselves. That the Socialism of Communism and Fascism is found everywhere among them all, from their swaddling clothes to their places of worship to their graves, serves to establish the fact they all are knowing servants of Lucifer and his minions. And I shall be hotter than Hell when I draw out my Great Sword after them to deprive them as they have sought deprivation upon the rest of mankind; and the Akurians after me shall continue to increase the agonies upon them until Shiloh.

268. "Sir, know that I will not spare any member or supporter or anyone who acts on behalf of the Bilderberger Organization, British Institute for International Affairs, Knights of Columbus, Masonic Lodge, Illuminati, Club of Rome, Temple

Israel, That Great Babylonian Harlot at Rome and all her Harlot Christian Daughters, Rockefeller Foundations, Rothchild Foundations, Trilateral Commission, Council on Foreign Relations, United Nations, World Bank, Fabian Society, Handgun Control, Inc., North American Free Trade Agreement **(NAFTA)**, North American Union **(NAU)**, General Agreement on Tariffs and Trade **(GATT)**, International Monetary Fund, Federal Reserve System, Marxists societies, United Kingdom Her Majesty's Treasury and Chancellors of the Exchequer, World Monetary Fund, World Council of Churches, World Health Organization and World Trade Organization, to name a very few. And I will not spare any Socialist government whether Marxist, Communist, Fascist, Socialist or Dictatorship.

269. "Sir, I am not impressed with the soulless racemixed Canaanite now sitting in the most powerful government seat in the whole world; and I have Cursed My Own Curse upon him and his administration and all who assisted in this Abomination of Damnation. He was put there by Socialists, uncounted lies, uncounted deceits, uncounted treasons, uncounted conspiracies, uncounted collusions and uncounted crimes. He is maintained there by Socialists and knowing media liars, primarily Kak Jews and Kak Jew-Puppets. That he will be expended by those same Socialists, Kak Jews and Kak Jew-Puppets when he has served his purpose is insufficient justice. That being said, the Hell I will bring down on the houses and the

heads of those same Socialists, Kak Jews and Kak Jew-Puppets will make up for any deficiencies.

270. "Sir, upon all their heads and all their houses shall I return the horrors they have set forth upon all others in their Abominations of Damnation. I will multiply those agonies by the same penalties I placed upon the Masonic Lodges and the Knights of Columbus in the days of my incarceration; and I will begin to account it against them from the hour of their instigation, be it minutes or be it millennia; and I will account it upon all their generations until Shiloh."

271. ""It is done.

272. ""The whole of the House of Levi, in whom I vested all Righteousness for mankind, and the Whole of the House of Judah, in whom My Servant Jacob vested the Septre of Identity that Israel not be lost unto the generations, are an abomination and a damnation and a disgust in My Sight. This day they are not My People; this day they are a disgrace in Israel; this day they have nothing righteous before Me; this day I accept their declaration as enemies they have chosen to be against Me. The whole of the House of Levi and the Whole of the House of Judah have conspired with That Great Babylonian Harlot at Rome and her Harlot Christian Daughters to enslave the whole world, and Ishmael is there among them. They hear Me not; neither do they consider My Prophet alive among them, except to mock and ridicule and suppress that My Truth be not sent

forth to all the Tribes, to all the Peoples and to all the Nations. Therefore, Son of My Great Wrath, pronounce upon them whatsoever you will, and I shall accomplish it unto the generations of Shiloh, and so shall it be judged against them in That Great Final Judgment.
273. ""Say you more against them?""

274. I answered, "Sir, knowing that none dare speak a lie in Your Presence, in Your Holy Presence and in the hearing of this entire gathering: I declare the Whole of the House of Levi, the Whole of the House of Judah, the Whole of the rest of the Children of Abraham including the Whole of the House of Ishmael, the Whole of That Great Babylonian Harlot at Rome and all her Harlot Christian Daughters, and all the Tribes of all the Gentiles to be worthy of all the Abominations of Damnation they have perpetrated; first, upon their own heads; and second, upon all the heads of all their generations after them until Shiloh.
275. "Sir, by the Righteous Power and Holy Authority of my Divine Office, I take all peace, security and comfort from them and send a multitude of violence, agony and death in place. That they all have perpetrated Abominations of Damnation upon their fellows and the whole world, their fellows and the whole world shall seek their blood and their bones in my Righteous Vengeance, the blade of my sword shall not spare them: from the unborn to the most aged, male and female,

whole and birth defected, rich and poor, free and bond, high born and common, clothed and naked, wise and foolish, great and unknown, weak and strong, far and near, armed and defenseless, well and afflicted, pure and diseased, powerful and powerless, worker and executive, skilled and unskilled, homosexual and heterosexual, fruitful and barren, atheist and believer, tall and squat, bloated and emaciated, in silk and in sackcloth; none shall escape and none shall deny.

276. "Sir, because all Socialism is the Greatest of All Abominations, committing Blasphemy Against the Holy Spirit of Truth by its very existence, I shall not spare them any agony, any disease, any affliction, any plague, any famine, nor any disaster that consumes without restraint and without mercy. These are some of the Marxist, both Communist and Fascist Socialist, entities and publications of whom none shall escape their own damnations I now turn against them: Bilderberger Organization, British Institute for International Affairs, Club of Rome, Council on Foreign Relations, Fabian Society, North American Free Trade Agreement, General Agreement on Tariffs and Trade, North American Union, Illuminati, International Monetary Fund, Handgun Control, Inc., Knights of Columbus, Masonic Lodge, Federal Reserve System, Marxists societies, Rockefeller Foundations, Rothchild Foundations, Trilateral Commission, United Kingdom Her Majesty's Treasury and Chancellors of the Exchequer, United Nations, World Bank, World Council of Churches,

THE BRIEFINGS PRIOR TO AND AUDIENCE BEFORE THE MOST HIGH

World Health Organization, World Trade Organization, Temple Israel, United States Supreme Court, United States House of Representatives, United States Senate, Change, Committee to Support the Revolution in Peru, Shining Path, Democratic Socialists of America, European Community Organisation of Socialist Youth, Association of Community Organizations for Reform Now, International Socialist Organization, Internationalist Group, Resistance **(Australia)**, Socialist Action, Socialist International, Virtual & Global Social Democratic Party, World Socialist Movement, Youth for International Socialism, Committee for a Workers' International, Douglas-Coldwell Foundation, Ernest Bevin Society, Fundacio Rafael Campalans, Göteborgs-kooperativet för Independent Living, International Committee of the Fourth International, Irish Republican Socialist Committee North America, News and Letters Women's Liberation Committee, Pressebuero Savanne, Queer Notions, RedLeaf, South Asia Solidarity Group, Workers World, Alliance for Workers' Liberty **(United Kingdom)**, Australian International Socialist Organisation, Democratic Socialist Party, Democratic Socialist Perspective **(Australia)**, Green Left Weekly, International Socialist Review, International Socialist Tendency, International Socialists **(Canada)**, New Socialist Group **(Canada)**, Socialist Alternative **(Australia)**, Socialist Organiser, Socialist Worker weekly, Socialist Workers Party, Australia's Socialist Alliance, Frontline, Imagine, International Socialist Movement (Scotland), International Socialist Organisation (Zimbabwe), Irish Republican Socialist Movement, Justice, Labor Militant, League for a Revolutionary Communist International, Official Irish Republican Army, Scottish Socialist Party, Socialist Action (U.S.), Socialist Alternative, Socialist Party of Canada, United Secretariat of the Fourth International, Workers Power, Workers' Power in Britain, Committee for a Workers International, Fight Back, Forward Motion, Freedom Road Socialist Organization, Kenya Socialist Democratic Alliance, Maavak Sozialisti (Israel), Socialist Democracy (Ireland), Socialist Viewpoint, Socialist Workers Organization (U.S.), International Communist League, International Socialist Organisation (Aotearoa, New Zealand), International Socialists (Scotland), Internationalist Group (U.S.), Socialist Appeal, Socialist Review, Spartacist League, Workers International League, Workers' Vanguard, Communist Workers Group New Zealand, International Socialist Organisation (Australia), League for the Fourth International, League of Revolutionaries for a New America, Liaison Committee of Militants for a Revolutionary Communist International, Red Action (United Kingdom), Workers Democratic Network, Communist Organization for the Fourth International, International Socialists, International Socialists Ireland, International Trotskyist Opposition (United Kingdom), League for the Revolutionary Party, Liaison Committee of Militants for a Revolutionary Communist International, Move-

THE BRIEFINGS PRIOR TO AND AUDIENCE BEFORE THE MOST HIGH

ment for a Socialist Future **(United Kingdom)**, Revolutionary Socialist League, Socialist Workers Party **(Ireland)**, Trotskyist League, Trotsky's Fourth International, Australian Egalitarian Movement Inc, Cannonite/International Committee, International Trotskyist Committee for the Political Regeneration of the Fourth International, Quaker Socialist Society, Real Union Of Social Science, Revolutionary Communist Group **(United Kingdom)**, Revolutionary Workers League/U.S, Socialism For A Real Labor Union, Socialist Alternative **(Ireland)**, Socialist Labor Party, World Socialist Network, and though this is not all those like these, I shall not permit any of the others any reprieve and the burning shall not be kept from them even beyond That Great Final Judgment. Let not any government of any Nation think itself immune, for they too are a part of the multitude of Damnations to Destructions. The Levites and the Jews among them are damned of direct guilt and all others who support them are damned of their own stupidity.

277. "Sir, and this is the beginning of the sorrows I shall inflict upon them that shall continue until Shiloh. My Curses of Damnations are like a viper in the night with neither warning nor rescue. And I curse them all: with war unlike all the destructions ever before and peace shall be nonexistent; with horrors unlike all the terrors to this time; with deprivations worse than all the scourges ever suffered; with pestilences greater than all the epidemics since the beginning; with decades of

drought; with storms and floods that will not become usable water; with fires in their growing seasons leaving only plagues, disease and famine; the United Nations global monetary system shall be a stink in the air without worth or prosperity; the noise of the One World Government's collapse shall be covered by the din and clatter of liars and murderers shouting its success; every pot shall be a cesspool; every bed a sop of dung and urine; every shelter shall be a feeding place of asymptomatics; every watchman shall be an honorless enemy; every sanctuary shall be a death trap; every table shall be a shelf of poison; every graveyard shall be a food cache and every sepulcher a larder; lice and ticks shall be a delicacy; that in a gripped fist shall be a hoard; and I am not yet finished.

278. "Sir, the stone of the field shall remove the Socialist, the Levite, the Jew and the Demon-possessed as a sacrifice to the Gods of War that there might be a moment of peace; the Gods of Enslavement that there might be a moment of relief; the Gods of Gold and Finance that there might be a moment of sustenance; the Gods of Epidemic Crime that there might be a moment of safety; the Gods of Ethnic Cleansing and Merciless Death that there might be a moment of life the Angels of Death do not deplore; the Gods of Endless Plagues that there might be a moment of healing, and the Gods of Great Famine that there might be a morsel of sustenance in that time. I declare condemnation upon the Whole of the House of Levi, the Whole of the House of Judah,

the Whole of the House of Ishmael, the Whole of That Great Babylonian Harlot at Rome and the Whole of all her Harlot Christian Daughters, for they have preferred the Gods of War, the Gods of Enslavement, the Gods of Gold, the Gods of Finance, the Gods of Epidemic Crime, the Gods of Ethnic Cleansing, the Gods of Merciless Death, the Gods of Endless Plagues and the Gods of Great Famine in direct and knowing violation of Holy Law, ""You shall have no other gods before Me."" Therefore shall I bless the stones of the field when the oppressed take the Socialist, the Levite, the Jew, the Catholic, the Christian and the Demon-possessed of Islam to the killing places of the land and slay them. Until they are all slain there shall not be any relief from their oppressions, their abominations nor their damnations upon the whole world. When the Gods who do not seek, nor accept, any following of their own before You, are satisfied the agony and the blood of the perpetrators is sufficient to fulfill the iniquity, and they bring their supplications to me, then and only then will I consider a lessening of their reproach.

279. "Sir, as a sign to all left standing in that hour, the Levite and the Jew shall paint their noses from between their eyes to the tip with ashes and soot to show their repentance to the people for all the oppressions, hardships and death they have brought upon them. The Catholic and the Harlot Christian shall paint their foreheads to show their repentance for the damnations they have brought upon themselves. The Muslims shall shave their

heads, both male and female, and men shall shave their beards, and they shall paint a mark from ear to ear over their head to show their repentance for all their violences and all the damnations they committed upon the world. The Gentiles shall paint the backs of their hands as a sign to all of their repentance and of their return to obedience to Holy Law to the exclusion of all other statutes and doctrines. When the Akurians see all these signs, and not one or two in a day here and three or four in a day there, but all of them everywhere in the same day, they may consider a good Testimony before You until Shiloh."

280. ""It is done.
281. ""Son of Fire, Son of My Good Pleasure: were Socialism not found anywhere upon the whole world; were the Children of Jacob, even Israel, restored to My Holy Statutes and refrained from slaying My Prophets among them; were the Children of Ishmael and all Islam awakened to My Holy Statutes and obey them at your hand; were That Great Babylonian Harlot at Rome and her Harlot Christian Daughters in accordance with My Holy Statutes as they claim to be and are not, the Gentiles would gather unto Me by those grand examples, I would have long ago removed Accursed Canaan from the face of the earth, and I would stay your hand and your Great Sword and your Great Righteous Powers and Holy Authorities that all these Justifications would not be. But none such is so, and I will not consider against you or

that which I am required to send you to do in My Sight. Therefore, My Beloved True and Righteous Akurians shall increase My Wrath and My Fury upon all offenders as shall seem good to them unto Shiloh. And none shall escape their Testimony.

282. ""Son of Fire, My Beloved Son of My Righteous Wrath, as there were once Elohim and Nefilim upon the earth, the whole world is rife with Demons and the self-inflicted Demon-possessed. Instructing you out of My Own Mouth in all things of your Holy Office, in the Days of your Preparations I sent you to see the world as it was then and as it is this very day; and your report was of Abominations of Damnations in the religions, in the synagogues, in the temples, in the churches, in the lodges, in the governments and all the institutions of man. In the Days of your Awakening and your Restoration to Knowledge, you did understand all these things and the evil of them and all their great unrighteousness. You learned the true causes, the true conspirators, the true perpetrators and the true essence of all these abominations before Me. And now those conspirators and perpetrators have ensnared the whole world into their clutches and into the stranglehold of the Great Demons.

283. ""Son of Fire, Beloved Sword of My Great Fury, that you are taught in My Presence and out of My Own Mouth is a great contention to all who will not hear My Voice because they are not of Me: the Whole of the House of Ishmael is deaf unto Me of Beelzebub; the Whole of the House of Israel is

deaf unto Me of their own damnations; the Whole of the Gentiles are deaf unto Me of their own ignorance; and of all of these, none are more deaf unto Me than the Whole of the House of Levi and the Whole of the House of Judah. That Great Babylonian Harlot at Rome and all her Harlot Christian Daughters hear me not because I speak not to any of them; neither are any of My Righteous Messengers **(Angels)** nor My True Servants **(humans)** found anywhere among them; I guide them not; all they profess of Me is an Abomination of Damnations, a gathering of lies and Blasphemy Against the Holy Spirit of Truth. They have chosen their other gods and I have nothing to do with them; they are not of Me nor any of Mine. That they are ensnared in their abominations is upon their own heads, for they maintain their ensnarement at their own hands.

284. ""Son of Fire, Beloved Sword of My Great Fury, that you are taught in My Presence and out of My Own Mouth is a great contention to the Whole of the House of Levi, who threw My Righteousness in the draught of the streets that it go the way of flowing dung. That you are taught in My Presence and out of My Own Mouth is a great contention to the Whole of the House of Judah who profess to be My Chosen People. And they are not! They are those who prefer the glitter of gold and the shine of silver to My Holy Statutes, and the power of wealth to Me. I am not their God because they are not My People. They have chosen the ways of the harlots and the harlotmongers, and

THE BRIEFINGS PRIOR TO AND AUDIENCE BEFORE THE MOST HIGH

there is no righteousness anywhere in them nor among them. Now you shall chasten them as My Rod of Iron, and I order you to spare them not.

285. ""Son of Fire, My Pride and My Joy in all the Earth, did I not say of you in the Days of the Repentance of David? Did I not tell it well of you? **(Psalms 2:1)** "Why do the heathen rage, and the people imagine a vain thing? **(2:2)** The kings of the earth set themselves, and the rulers take counsel together, against The Lord, and against His Anointed, saying, **(2:3)** "Let us break their bands asunder, and cast away their cords from us." **(2:4)** He that sits in the heavens shall laugh: The Lord shall have them in derision. **(2:5)** Then shall He speak unto them in His Wrath, and vex them in His sore displeasure. **(2:6)** Yet have I set My King upon My Holy Hill of Zion. **(2:7)** I will Declare the Decree: The Lord hath said unto me, Thou art My Son; this day have I begotten thee. **(2:8)** Ask of me, and I shall give thee the heathen for thine inheritance, and the uttermost parts of the earth for thy possession. **(2:9)** Thou shalt break them with a rod of iron; thou shalt dash them in pieces like a potter's vessel. **(2:10)** Be wise now therefore, O ye kings: be instructed, ye judges of the earth. **(2:11)** Serve The Lord with fear, and rejoice with trembling. **(2:12)** Kiss the Son, lest he be angry, and ye perish from the way, when his wrath is kindled but a little. Blessed are all they that put their trust in him."

286. ""Son of Fire, My Holy and Anointed Son of My Own Righteousness, know that I spoke of

none other, neither David nor Immanuel, neither any priest nor any calling themselves of My Name; but of you alone upon whom I named My Own Name, ALIHA ASUR HIGH.

287. ""Son of Fire, My Own Anointed King of Zion: the heathen rage, people imagine vain things, the kings and rulers have taken counsel together and set themselves against Me and against You, My Anointed. Do they not think their Gods of Wealth and Power of Wealth have broken all the embindments of My Holy Statutes? Yea! And they commit wholesale robbery upon all the Nations! Yea! They think themselves to be above the law because they are the law at their seducing of the people. I laugh at their vanities, at their ignorances, and at their inability to delay My Wrath and their inability to soften My Rod of Iron. I have warned them, and I have warned them all; the Great Warning in the company of Masons and Knights of the Lodges at Pendleton; and this too they did ignore: nevertheless, that day did I beget you as My Own and Only Anointed Son **(27th June, 1962 – 25 Sivan 5722)**. I asked of you to ask of Me, and you wanted nothing, not even the heathen for a possession. I warned them you would break them with a Rod of Iron and to smash them as terracotta, and I warned them to cease foolishness and take your Teachings of Righteousness and not to offend you; but they have laughed in their own derision of Me, My Holy Statutes, you, and your Holy Office before Me. Blessed shall be all those who have The Great

THE BRIEFINGS PRIOR TO AND AUDIENCE BEFORE THE MOST HIGH

Testimony and those who heed your teachings and obey your commands and orders; but to all others spare not your anger, and whatsoever you shall put upon them, I shall multiply the agony thereof. Spare them not.
288. ""Say you more against them?""

289. I answered, "Sir, I have not found any true patriots anywhere in the United States Congress or Governing Agencies. None. All are without excuse, for they have all violated their Oath of Office sworn before you and the people, saying "So help me, God!" and they ignored Your help in that same instant and their Oath of Office, "I do solemnly swear **(or affirm)** that I will faithfully execute the office of President of the United States, and will to the best of my ability, preserve, protect and defend the Constitution of the United States," as President; and "I do solemnly swear **(or affirm)** that I will support and defend the Constitution of the United States against all enemies, foreign and domestic; that I will bear true faith and allegiance to the same; that I take this obligation freely, without any mental reservation or purpose of evasion; and that I will well and faithfully discharge the duties of the office on which I am about to enter: So help me, God" for Congress; and noting the "against all enemies, foreign and domestic" in the next.
290. "Sir, I thank you for the opportunity, presented and available to everyone, to serve the Cause of Righteousness, to know and understand

and obey Holy Law, to hear Your Voice, to know Your Presence, and to deny all evil. That I chose as I did of my own free will, the mistakes I have made are upon my head alone, and my repentance and servitude have brought me to great recognitions throughout all Creation and brought great Honor upon my House of Din. I take full responsibility for myself and all my decisions and all my actions. There is nobody else at fault for my failures, and nobody else responsible for my successes. That I have had good advice is nothing exceptional; good and righteous advice is available to all who will seek it with an open and prudent mind. Therefore, when You advised the Kings and Rulers, there was not then, and there is not now, any greater or truer righteous advice. They chose to ignore You and Holy Law of themselves; they chose to ignore and abuse Your Anointeds, including me, of themselves; and their conspiracies and collusions shall not be accounted upon them piece by piece and who by who, but the Whole of the damnations upon each and every head as though each were the only one. I will make the Rod of Iron seem as a flitting flower petal by comparison; each and every one of them shall beg for a return to the Rod of Iron as an act of mercy and relief. And I and my Akurians shall abide them the exact same mercy and relief they have shown those who resisted them, the Tribes, the Peoples and the Nations: *None at all!* They deserve none and none they will get, until Shiloh.

THE BRIEFINGS PRIOR TO AND AUDIENCE BEFORE THE MOST HIGH

291. "Sir, of those who spared no effort to rob the Nations and the People of the Nations of all their wealth and worth: John Anderson, Anthony Ashley-Cooper, Francis Baring, Edward Barrett, William Barrington, Hicks Beach, Robert Benson, Ben Shalom Bernanke, Thomas Browne, George Canning, William Catesby, Eugene Robert Black, Henry Booth, John Bourchier, Herbert Asquith, John Baker, Gordon Brown, John Cavendish, Austen Chamberlain, Neville Chamberlain, Hugh Childers, Randolph Churchill, Stanley Baldwin, Anthony Perrinott Lysberg Barber, Arthur Frank Burns, Francis Cottington, Richard Stafford Cripps, Daniel Richard Crissinger, Edward Hugh John Neale Dalton, Alistair Darling, Richard Austen Butler, Julius Caesar, William Dowdeswell, John Duncombe, Denis Ealey, Marriner Stoddard Eccles, John Ernle, Winston Spencer Churchill, John Foster, Hugh Todd Naylor Gaitskell, Ralph Gore, George Goschen, Henry Goulburn, Leonard James Callaghan, Charles Abbott, David Lloyd George, Alan Greenspan, George Grenville, Fulke Greville, Henry Addington, John Aislabie, William Vernon Harcourt, Charles Sumner Hamlin, Richard Hampden, William Proctor Gould Harding, Robert Harley, Kenneth Clarke, William Gerard Hamilton, George Home, John Charles Herries, Michael Hicks Beach, Edward Hyde, Roy Harris Jenkins, Robert Horne, Richard Jones, Richard Edward Geoffrey Howe, Norman Lamont, Andrew Bonar Law, George Ward Hunt, Henry Bilson Legge, George Cornewall Lewis, John

AKURIAN METAPHYSICAL HANDBOOK
VOLUME I

Colepeper, Iain MacLeod, Maurice Harold Macmillan, Selwyn Lloyd, John Roy Major, Isaac Corry, Francis Dashwood, John Fortescue, Reginald McKenna, Eugene Isaac Meyer, Walter Mildmay, George William Miller, Benjamin Disraeli, Denis Winston Healey, Derick Heathcoat-Amory, Nigel Lawson, William Lee, Thomas Bayard McCabe, Frederick North, Stafford Northcote, Richard Onslow, Henry Pelham, Charles T. Ritchie, Frederick John Robinson, Robert Lowe, Thomas Spring Rice, John Simon, George Lyttelton, William McChesney Martin, Jr., John Smith, Charles Montagu, George Edward Peter Thorneycroft, William Murray, Godfrey Giffard, Paul Adolph Volcker, William Gladstone, Henry Boyle, Thomas Denman, Reginald Maudling, Robert Peel, Samuel Sandys, William Wyndham, Spencer Perceval, William Wellesley-Pole, John Spencer, Richard Weston, Charles Wood, Henry Petty-Fitzmaurice, William Pitt, John Pratt, Philip Snowden, Hervey De Stanton, Charles Townshend, Nicholas Vansittart, William Vesey-Fitzgerald, Robert Walpole, Roy Archibald Young, Kingsley Wood, James Stanhope, and all the Kings and Queens and Rulers over them; and all their fellows including all those of the various Treasuries, and all their servants, and all their respective generations after them, I now remove all peace and every good thing from them and sentence them to Die the Death and Burn in the Horrors until Shiloh.

292. "Sir, that many are already dead and burning does not alter my sentence of greater damnation and suffering upon them. That many more will sit in their seats and commit Abominations of Damnations without restraint or righteous consideration, I also direct that any victim may avenge themselves by directing "Aku curse you" toward any or all of them at any time. If that invocation is invoked upon one already dead, it will increase the Burning in the Horrors; if that invocation is directed toward a grave or a sepulcher and the corpse is not there, the increase of Burning in the Horrors shall not diminish, that none escape their just due. And Hell itself shall be afrightened when that invocation comes from any Akurian, and Lucifer will seek the Infernal Dungeons when that invocation comes from any True and Righteous Proven Knower of The Great Testimony, knowing it applies to him and all his minions too.

293. "Sir, as respecting any and all United States' political parties: all are liars and knowing traitors to the House of Ephraim. I set but one example in This Audience: the Republican Party, of which all candidates claim "Republican core values" condemning themselves out of their own mouths and by their own actions. The Patriot Act, Military Commissions Act, Gun Control and the Troubled Asset Relief Program **(TARP)** bailout are not "Republican core values" by any stretch of the imagination, but they are all damned well heavily plated in Marxism, Communism, Fascism and One

World Government. The first three are nothing more than legislated enslavement; and TARP is intended solely to openly extort the entire resources of the Nation and to the ultimate detriment of the whole world. That such Abomination of Damnations came as much from Republicans as it did Democrats, Independents and Socialists is no surprise, since all are knowing puppets of the Bilderbergers and such Demonic Organizations. They may be many, voters included, but none shall escape the Hell soon to be poured over their worthless, treasonous asses."

294. ""It is done.

295. ""Son of Fire, My Own Anointed Teacher of True Righteousness, the religions, the temples, the synagogues, the churches and the lodges are filled with Demons teaching only Doctrines of Death; racemixing is a diseased-dung cesspool, and children are polluted in the womb and desecrated from birth. My Holy Statutes are used only to hide behind when the vile and the corrupt are brought into the open light. They whine love and forgiveness, mercy and toleration they never shew to any of their victims, including you and My Beloved Akurians.

296. ""Son of Fire, Lord of Lords of all the Orders of Powers, the religions neither hear nor know anything of My Holy Statutes and the Great Spiritual Mysteries thereof. By the same Righteous Powers and Holy Authorities Immanuel raised the proven dead did you and Daughter of

THE BRIEFINGS PRIOR TO AND AUDIENCE BEFORE THE MOST HIGH

Akuria Dianne Chylon Budagher bring forth the millions of millions of the spirits of the dead; and the religions knew it not, neither did they honor the accomplishment.

297.   ""Son of Fire, Lord of Lords of all the Orders of Authorities, the temples are as dung hills and abominations upon their foundations in My Sight. They dress in simple garb to present the face of secret holiness and teach grand-sounding nonsense as a superior lifestyle; and glorify him whom I sent as a testimony against them **(Muhammad)**. And only the fools listen or pay them any homage. They have nothing of value either secret or open, and My Holy Due squandered into their hands is a Great Abomination unto Me, for it is a knowing and deliberate desecration upon that which I would have made Righteous.

298.   ""Son of Fire, Lord of Lords of all the Orders of Thrones, the synagogues are an abomination in Israel. Professing great righteousness, they are the worst of liars and the worst of thieves and the worst of traitors to the lands where I have dispersed them. They present their finest to impress and intimidate any lesser, they whine their oppression and innocence in their hypocrisy of oppressing the innocent more than all others upon the whole earth. And they fool only themselves against the time of their iniquity.

299.   ""Son of Fire, Lord of Lords of all the Orders of Dominions, the churches are filled with Demons, self-righteousness, spiritual ignorance

and Demonic damnations, heralding only Doctrines of Death. They sing hymns to nobody, yell sermons instantly ignored, beg much due squandered immediately, and howl their delusions as befits the prevailing perception. Lo! They are vile and vain congregations of Satanic glorifications, and Doctrines of Eternal Damnations.

300. ""Son of Fire, Lord of Lords of all the Orders of Principalities, the lodges are a vague religion of nothing of substance and of less honor. They rowdy and ramble, scheme and conspire, hail their brethren, and condemn all who stand not among them. They are no less hypocrites than the Levites and the Jews in their concoctions. Their rites are Demonic and knowing desecrations because they know their own lies and their own unrighteousness, reeking with the stink of the blood and bones of those rightly and wrongly convicted, grasping the graft instead of demanding true justice.

301. ""Son of Fire, Lord of Lords of all the Orders of Virtues, the races of man I saw fit to make and give life have seen fit to pollute themselves into lesser creatures than the beasts of the wilderness. They seek the empty pleasures of people of pretense, who present a multitude of personalities and are really none of them. The children are corrupted to blindly adore the vile and the painted and the empty, seeking destruction, imitating fiction, knowing little, understanding nothing, thinking not, and to whom wisdom is nonexistent.

THE BRIEFINGS PRIOR TO AND AUDIENCE BEFORE THE MOST HIGH

The children are as the sins of their fathers **(and mothers)**.

302. ""Son of Fire, Lord of Lords of all the Orders of All the Angels, the moralities I established in each and every living soul has evaporated as a light dew in a hot morning, fathers and mothers raping and abusing their children, encouraging them into the dispicables of narcotics, crime, homosexuality and racemixing: the vilest of all Abominations of Damnation. Many are harmed, many are vile, most are lost and will not be redeemed. I will not have it so; therefore, call upon the Great Winds and bring the Rod of Iron of My Great Wrath upon the whole world until every knee bow to My Authority, and every tongue confess My Greatness above all, and every soul honor My Holy Ones.

303. ""Son of Fire, Lord of Lords in All the Heavens Above All the Earths, Holy Prophet of Abraham, prophesy against the religions; against the temples; against the synagogues; against the churches; against the lodges; against the races; against the homosexuals and all who create, cause, support and perpetuate the Abominations of Damnation that they escape nothing at your hand.

304. ""Say you more against them?""

305. I answered, "Sir, all these things are true and none of them are hidden from even the most isolated mind. They are all open and overt in the daylight and in the dark; they are everywhere in the streets and blazed constantly by all the media.

Schools are crime and drug-infested war zones; highways and streets are concrete strips of terror; news, information and entertainment are but issuances of moral filth, lies and Socialism; governments are armed enemies of and against unarmed and defenseless citizens; food and water are poisons for the sake of pennies; market goods are expensive trash; services are scams in all descriptions; honor and integrity are but claims of lying, murdering politicians and appointed puppets; and truth is Blasphemed without ceasing.

306. "Sir, sometimes there is little sunshine and less rain in due season.

307. "Sir, knowing that none dare speak a lie in Your Presence, in Your Holy Presence and in the hearing of this entire gathering: My Greater Condemnation and binding in all the Heavens above all the Earths, in all the Earths, and in all the Depths beneath all the Earths is and shall remain a Curse of Curses of Great Agonies and Burning in the Horrors upon the Whole of the House of Levi and the Whole of the House of Judah for all their Abominations of Damnation, their continuous lies and their thieveries and their desecrations. Sir, knowing that none dare speak a lie in Your Presence, in Your Holy Presence and in the hearing of this entire gathering, I adjudicate the Whole of the House of Levi, the Sons of Aaron, the Whole of the House of Judah and the Whole of Zionism guilty of all Socialism and direct and knowing violation of all Holy Law. If I have said any falsehood against any here, living or dead upon the

earth, including the Prophets Enoch and Elijah, now here in This Presence and incarnate with the Nefilim, speak against me that all be upon my head alone."

308. The Most High remained silent.

309. "Sir, knowing that none dare speak a lie in Your Presence, in Your Holy Presence and in the hearing of this entire gathering: My Greater Condemnation and binding in all the Heavens above all the Earths, in all the Earths, and in all the Depths beneath all the Earths is and shall remain a Curse of Curses of Great Agonies and Burning in the Horrors upon the Whole of the House of Ishmael, and all who follow and tolerate the Muslim Tradition, for all their Abominations of Damnation, their continuous lies and their thieveries and their desecrations and their forced acceptances of Islam in direct and knowing violation of all Holy Law. Sir, knowing that none dare speak a lie in Your Presence, in Your Holy Presence and in the hearing of this entire gathering, I adjudicate the Whole of the House of Ishmael, and all who follow and tolerate the Muslim Tradition, guilty of direct and knowing violation of all Holy Law, for they torture their women, deceive their children, and murder innocents for the sake of murder, claiming all to be justified and holy. All who practice and all who condone such are knowing liars and hypocrites possessed of Beelzebub, and they are knowing and willing servants of Beelze-

bub and Lucifer even as their many minions. If I have said any falsehood against any here, living or dead upon the earth, speak against me that all be upon my head alone."

310. The Most High remained silent.

311. "Sir, knowing that none dare speak a lie in Your Presence, in Your Holy Presence and in the hearing of this entire gathering: My Greater Condemnation and binding in all the Heavens above all the Earths, in all the Earths, and in all the Depths beneath all the Earths is and shall remain a Curse of Curses of Great Agonies and Burning in the Horrors upon the Whole of That Great Babylonian Harlot at Rome and all her Harlot Christian Daughters for all their Abominations of Damnation, their continuous lies and their thieveries and their desecrations and their knowing and deliberate deceptions of claimed truth and righteousness in the face of contrary Holy Law and the Great Commandments. Sir, knowing that none dare speak a lie in Your Presence, in Your Holy Presence and in the hearing of this entire gathering, I adjudicate the Whole of That Great Babylonian Harlot at Rome and all her Harlot Christian Daughters guilty of direct and knowing violation of all Holy Law and being willingly possessed and deceived by every Demon: Lucifer, Abbadona, Astarothae (Iblis), Baalberith, Beelzebub, Behemoth, Belphegor, Forcas, Leviathan, Mammon, Shemhazai and Xaphan and all their

minions, excepting Urakabarameel and Aeshmodeva whom I slew in Your Presence, and whose minions remain for the Great Possessing. If I have said any falsehood against any here, living or dead upon the earth, speak against me that all be upon my head alone."

312. The Most High remained silent.

313. "Sir, knowing that none dare speak a lie in Your Presence, in Your Holy Presence and in the hearing of this entire gathering: I charge and indict Lucifer who is not present and all his minions who are present, Abbadona, Astarothae, Baalberith, Beelzebub, Behemoth, Belphegor, Forcas, Leviathan, Mammon, Shemhazai and Xaphan and all their minions, including the minions of Urakabarameel, and Aeshmodeva, some of whom are present, with knowing and deliberate possessing of the ignorant and the innocent and bringing the Penalties of all Abominations and Damnations upon those unknowing and unsuspecting souls. Sir, knowing that none dare speak a lie in Your Presence, in Your Holy Presence and in the hearing of this entire gathering, I adjudicate the Whole of the Congregation of Demons guilty of all I say against them. And I say to one and to all of them, here and now, 'If I have spoken anything against you that is not Truth Eternal Before The Most High,' speak against me now and bring your unsheathed slaying weapon that I may justifiably slay you before the time."

314. All the Demons remained silent in the Face of The Most High's defiant one.

315. "Sir, knowing that none dare speak a lie in Your Presence, in Your Holy Presence and in the hearing of this entire gathering: I charge and indict all Socialists with and for all godlessness and all knowing lies, deceptions of the ignorant and destruction of the innocent. I charge and indict all the Supreme Courts of the Whole of the United States with and for being Marxists, Communists, Fascists, Socialists, knowing traitors, protectors of corrupt police, direct advocates of money laundering to increase and enhance the plague of narcotics in the streets and of the pharmaceutical companies, and declaring a soulless and Marxist Canaanite to be President of these United States without his presentation of proper and adequate documentation of his right and authorization to serve in that office. My charges and indictments against the United States Supreme Court and all lesser courts of the land are all these things and many more without exception. All Justices of the Supreme Court of the United States are no less criminals than all the organized and unorganized criminals found everywhere else in the world. Hear me, all Akuria: In each and every instance you encounter any Socialist and any Socialist Agenda regardless of the disguise, including corrupt police, corrupt politicians and the Black Robed Bastards on any bench of any court, in that instance invoke a new layer of Hell

upon them and their generations after them until Shiloh, and spare them not. Their lies, their robberies, their treasons, their murders and spiritual abominations are the most vile of the vilest: Spare them not! Hear me, all Children of Abraham: You are required to be pure in your generations, even as Father Abraham is pure in his generations of Ish and through Noah. You cannot remove or even reduce the Great Curses upon Canaan, Cush and the Gentiles by any process except bringing them to Holy Law by your own good example. And how can you know them in this corrupt and polluted generation? By clean observation. In their cry for recognition that they are alive and suffer the same hungers, abuses, deprivations and abominations as all others seem not to suffer, they will dress themselves in the gooniest of raiment, conduct themselves in the most extreme and obnoxious manner, and hide their cowardice behind gang numbers. Whoever is like this anywhere at any time, you know you have encountered a Canaanite, unrepentant Cushite or a spiritually ignorant Gentile. And know for a certainty, that when the Nefilim are required to return and restore the whole world and the whole earth, they will first slaughter each and every cell of Canaan, and spare only the repentant Cushites of all the Black Races. Hear me, all Earth: the Days of Horror for your own damnations are this side of the horizon.

316. "Sir, by the Righteous Powers and Holy Authorities of My Holy Office of Anointed Messiah of this Generation of Ish, I call Seven

Archangels and twelve Angels in This Audience and of This Holy Presence and the Eight Winds of Creation:

317. "Sir, I summon Archangel Raphael, Standing in His Place of Honor in This Audience, Ruler of the First Quarter of Air, Master of the East Wind Apelotes, whose Servant is the Wind Eurea under ever faithful Bahaliel [ba-HAL-e-EL], Servant of The Most High Lord God of All Creation, ALIHA ASUR HIGH; I call upon Holy Sarabotes [sar-a-BO-tes], Chief of the Angels of Air, bring forth all your energies, forces, powers and authorities: who shall deny me not!

318. "Sir, I summon Archangel Michael, Standing in His Place of Honor in This Audience, Ruler of the Second Quarter of Fire, Master of the South Wind Notae, whose Servant is the Wind Lipae [LI-pay] under ever faithful Nafriel [NAY-fri-EL], Servant of The Most High Lord God of All Creation, ALIHA ASUR HIGH; I call upon Holy Jehuel [yeh-WHO-EL], Chief of the Angels of Fire, bring forth all your energies, forces, powers and authorities: who shall deny me not!

319. "Sir, I summon Archangel Gabriel, Standing in His Place of Honor in This Audience, Ruler of the Third Quarter of Water, Master of the West Wind Zephyros, whose Servant is the Wind Skiron [SKY-ron] under ever faithful Aniel [a-NI-el], Servant of The Most High Lord God of All Creation, ALIHA ASUR HIGH; I call upon Holy Hamal [HAY-mile], Chief of the Angels of Water,

bring forth all your energies, forces, powers and authorities: who shall deny me not!

320. "Sir, I summon Archangel Uriel, Standing in His Place of Honor in This Audience, Ruler of the Fourth Quarter of Earth, Master of the North Wind Boreas, whose Servant is the Wind Kaikias [kay-KI-us] under ever faithful Beli [BEL-i], Servant of The Most High Lord God of All Creation, ALIHA ASUR HIGH; I call upon Holy Forlok [FOR-lock], Chief of the Angels of Earth, bring forth all your energies, forces, powers and authorities: who shall deny me not!

321. "Sir, I summon Archangel Remiel, Standing in His Place of Honor in This Audience, Ruler of All the Binding in All the Heavens Above All the Earths, and in All the Earths, and in All the Depths Beneath All the Earths: binding all the authorities of Ben Nez [ben-NEZ], Guard of the Main Gates of the East Wind; binding all the authorities of Pruel [pru-EL], Guard of the Main Gates of the West Wind; binding all the authorities of Druiel [dru-e-EL], Guard of the Main Gates of the South Wind; binding all the authorities of Albim [al-BI-m], Guard of the Main Gates of the North Wind; and binding all the authorities of Yhodukah [hew-du-KAH], Servant of The Most High Lord God of All Creation, ALIHA ASUR HIGH: who shall deny me not!

322. "Sir, I summon Archangel Raguel, Standing in His Place of Honor in This Audience, Ruler of the Loosening in All the Heavens Above All the Earths, and in All the Earths, and in All the Depths

Beneath All the Earths: loosening all the powers of Ben Nez, Guard of the Main Gates of the East Wind; loosening all the powers of Pruel, Guard of the Main Gates of the West Wind; loosening all the powers of Druiel, Guard of the Main Gates of the South Wind; loosening all the powers of Albim, Guard of the Main Gates of the North Wind; and loosening all the powers of Yhodukah; Servant of The Most High Lord God of All Creation, ALIHA ASUR HIGH: who shall deny me not!

323. "Sir, I summon Archangel Zerachiel, Standing in His Place of Honor in This Audience, First Guardian of All the Holy Anointed Witnesses in Their Generations, Communicator Between The Holy Altar and the Ark of the Covenant of The Most High, Servant of The Most High Lord God of All Creation, ALIHA ASUR HIGH: who shall deny me not!

324. "Sir, above all others I Curse each and every Socialist and all Socialism regardless of intent or title. I have found no greater Abomination of Damnation than the Demon-possessed and ignorance-inflicted victims of Socialism, producing more degeneracies than the practices of the Nefilim, more atrocities than That Great Babylonian Harlot at Rome and all her Harlot Christian Daughters, and creating more immoralities than all other religions and political systems combined, except the neglect and Abandonment of the Priests of Levi. A greater Damnation of Damnations do I embind until Shiloh upon each and every Socialist, for they promise much to gain power, and once

empowered, deliver nothing but infinite and merciless control, enforcing their authorities with death and destruction and will not willingly remove themselves. Therefore, my Curse of Curses will infest and infect all Socialism, expanding its damnations with hardships until the very sewers cry out for relief and gladly accept the residue of dead Socialists wherever they are slain. Every hand shall gather a slaying stone and will not spare any Socialist nor any who enforce any Socialist Agenda. And the Akurians will never permit any Socialist to achieve lasting comfort or escape of punishment for their atrocities over the mind of man nor their many murders. The Testimony of all Akurians shall be against all Socialism and Socialists and all their generations after them until Shiloh.

325. "Sir, I Curse each and every religion that preaches any message other than full adherence to Holy Law without exception. I will not excuse any other doctrine; I will not excuse any explanation; I will not excuse any delusion; I will not excuse any disguise; and I will not excuse any Demon. I bind their damnations upon them and their generations after them until Shiloh, and all who are deceived of them shall increase the burning of that religion.

326. "Sir, I curse each and every False Doctrine of each and every religion, especially and without exception the Abomination of Damnations of That Great Babylonian Harlot at Rome for all her rapes, child murders and child sacrifices; her Demonic-damnation of constantly crossing themselves to

embind their souls with Eternal Death in their ignorance regardless of what the congregations are taught; her perpetual rambling of beads and reciting damnations upon their own heads and upon all who are intended; and the Abomination of Desecration upon Mariah and Immanuel, and ordaining Saints which they have neither power nor authority to do. The death of any Catholic and any Christian shall begin with Burning in the Horrors and there they shall remain until Final Judgment.

327. "Sir, I Curse each and every temple without exception; where there is no True Righteousness there is nothing but deception, degradation, Demons and destruction: the raiment, the waters, the oils, the wines, the incense, the candles, the bells, the gongs, the whistles, the flutes, the horns, the drums, the strings, the chants, the songs, the prayers, the sacrifices, the dues, the gifts, the offerings, the blessings, the rituals, the foods, the drinks, the trappings, the regalia, the symbols, the statuary, the books, the scrolls, the pictures, the images, the manuscripts, the staff and all the activities are forever an Abomination of Damnations and a desecration and a Blasphemy Against the Holy Spirit of Truth. Damned they are and Damned they shall remain in all their generations until Shiloh.

328. "Sir, I Curse each and every synagogue without exception, for they are the lair of abominations of Levi and damnations of Judah. From the Hour of Justification: their observations shall

be a useless and expensive burden, their holy water shall be as drunken piss, their holy oil shall be as anus lubricant, their holy wine shall be as diseased menstruation, and the breath of their chants and prayers shall be as the dregs of soured cess. The Great and Irrevocable Curse Upon the Whole of the House of Levi and the Great and Irrevocable Curse Upon the Whole of the House of Judah shall be rehearsed against them every hour until Shiloh.

329. "Sir, I Curse each and every church of That Great Babylonian Harlot at Rome and all her Harlot Christian Daughters for their perpetual Blasphemes Against You, The Most High; their perpetual Blasphemes Against the Holy Spirit of Truth; their perpetual Blasphemes Against all Holy Law; their perpetual Blasphemes Against My Brother Horseman Immanuel whom they knowingly incorrectly call 'Jesus;' and their perpetual Blasphemes against His Righteous mother, Mariah, whom they constantly defame as 'mother of god.' I pronounce a Damnation of Damnations upon each and every servant of their congregations for their rapes and ritual murders and all their deliberate enforcements of the Doctrines of Death; and the many horrors and agonies upon them shall make the very dirt under their feet to seem unjust. And I shall not relieve them nor any of their generations after them until Shiloh.

330. "Sir, I Curse each and every lodge professing any restricted or secret information, whether a sign, a password, a handshake or any other

instruction. They are but conspirators against the innocent and therefore are undeserving of life. From the Hour of Justification they shall suffer my Curse of Curses upon all their members and all their fellows and all their men and all their women and all their children; for they breathe to pollute and destroy my planet, all justice on my planet, and all True Righteousness wherever they sojourn. They shall know greater deprivation and injustice than all their victims. I will not have mercy and neither will My Great Curse of Curses upon them spare any of them or of theirs.

331. "Sir, I Curse each and every racemixer; excusing only the truly repentant of Cush. That racemixing should not be done in Israel is ancient and Holy Law; that racemixing should not be done in any Tribe is the foundation of True Righteousness upon the people. Therefore, whosoever is a racemixer, let them repent now, before the Hour of Justification; and whosoever shall advocate racemixing among any Tribes, any Peoples, or any Nations, I shall visit the harshest of persecutions upon them and all their generations after them forever. Advocates and racemixers alike shall be slain in the streets, slaughtered in the darkness, branded as livestock that their abominations be known to all, rejected by all of right morals, and in That Day be removed, even as the Canaanite, from all the Houses of The Most High.

332. "Sir, I Curse every vile and degenerate homosexual, and withhold all damnation from the harmed. I will not spare any who has created a

harmed. The vile such as Rosie O'Donnell, Ellen DeGeneres, Harvey Bernard Milk and United States House Representative Barnett "Barney" Frank (D-MA) are worthy only of Eternal Burning. Harvey Bernard Milk is already burning and screaming his promises to *'go back and tell the others'* that fall on deaf ears. The deepest firepits of Hell await the rest and all others like them. They are all glorified to the highest reaches by Socialist Media; but My Great Curse of Curses upon them invoked in This Very Audience shall bring them all down to the Deepest of All the Depths of Eternal Burning, along with all their fellows and all their advocates of whatsoever manner, and all their respective generations after them until Shiloh.

333. "Sir, I Curse each and every human who shall abuse any child, whether in the womb, in the home or in the sanctuaries. Children are the Treasure of Tomorrow and the hope of mankind's eventual redemption; therefore, children are a sacred trust. I know the child rapes and abuses of the Whole of the House of Levi and the Whole of the House of Judah; and I know the child rapes and murders of That Great Babylonian Harlot at Rome and her Harlot Christian Daughters; and My Great Curse of Curses upon them shall avenge each and every victim and burn each and every perpetrator. I will not excuse any, not the perpetrator and not the parent or guardian who shall permit any child to enter into any Domicile of Demons and the Doctrines of Death.

334. "Sir, I call forth Archangel Raphael, the East Wind Apelotes, the Wind Eurea, Bahaliel, Sarabotes, Archangel Michael, the South Wind Notae, the Wind Lipae, Nafriel, Jehuel, Archangel Gabriel, the West Wind Zephyros, the Wind Skiron, Aniel, Hamal, Archangel Uriel, the North Wind Boreas, the Wind Kaikias, Beli, Forlok, Archangel Remiel, Ben Nez, Pruel, Druiel, Albim, Archangel Raguel and Archangel Zerachiel and charge them with making My Curse of Curses, and all that I and any Akurian shall add thereto, manifest in Earth and upon the whole world until Shiloh.

335. "Sir, I have blessed the True and Righteous, cursed the unrighteous, challenged all the Demons and warned the whole world. Is there more You require of me?"

336. ""It is done.

337. ""Son of Fire, go now in Great Honor for your work is nearly finished, and not even the Gates of all the Depths of Hell can prevail against it.

338. ""Whosoever has ears to hear, let them hear and listen; whosoever has eyes to see, let them see and observe the damnations in their presence and the times of tribulations upon the whole world. None can listen and none can observe and not know and understand all these things are of Me; and I will not repent of one jot or tittle until all be fulfilled.

339. ""Write it in a book and deliver it to all who will accept this revelation.

THE BRIEFINGS PRIOR TO AND AUDIENCE BEFORE THE MOST HIGH

340. **""It is written, it is finished.""**

341. That eventually Hell will consume all the vile and unrighteous, includes every Socialist whether a great historical leader or a fool of the common populace. Understand for a never-changing fact, the Akurians don't care "what" anybody 'believes' or what they 'think they know' as a matter of religion, politics or anything else. Either you are living in obedience to and accordance with Holy Law as given in the Torah as it applies to you, or you are not. If you are, you're qualified to be an Akurian, regardless of race, education, et cetera; if not, you are certainly included above. Therefore, to all fools, from the highest and lowest, including all those involved in organized crime, medical malfeasance, other public deprivations or animal abuse who think I overlooked you or your damnations: pay close attention, *I did not!* I even included all ancestors who fell short of the Holy Law mark, starting with my own.

342. **The Most High, Himself, Testifies that each and every word, statement and claim in this book is infinite, absolute, irrevocable, consistently verifiable Truth.**

343. To repeat ourselves: **If The Testimony of The Most High, Himself, isn't sufficient,** *what would be?*

344. A point for all remaining history: compiling and editing this report into English required the

effort and input of several people; some mentioned in the various volumes of **"The ANOINTED, The ELECT, and The DAMNED!"** and other Akurian writings, scripts, articles, lessons and news releases, and some not. Those who contributed the most are Command Marshal General D. Chylon Budagher, P.K., Staff General Rosalind R. Clark, P.K. and Brigadier General Kathryn A. Malone, P.K. Without these three Holy and Righteous Daughters of Akuria, who are also Holy and Righteous Daughters of Elisha, this report would not be possible in this time frame between the New Moon beginning of this Hour of Justification and publication.

El Aku ALIHA ASUR HIGH.

THE AKURIAN HOLY OATH

Upon my head, and upon the head of my generations after me, in All the Heavens and in All the Earths: do I vow and commit My Sacred Honor to serve The Most High in all His Holy Establishments, to obey His officers over me, to resist treason against them, to punish insubordination and sedition immediately, to avow upon myself the horrors of eternal punishment greater than that upon any other, longer than that upon any other.

Let it be written, let it be done, upon me and all my generations after me if I fail!""

THE BRIEFINGS PRIOR TO AND AUDIENCE BEFORE THE MOST HIGH

EPILOG
Invitation to all Seekers of Truth

345. For those caught in the Damnations of The Most High: whether Hebrew, Cushite or Canaanite, Catholic, Christian, Moslim, Hindu, Gentile, Atheist, Satanist, 'psychic' (real or wannabe), or Seeker of Truth toward being a Master Metaphysician or Spiritualist; there is absolution and redirection of and from The Most High, Himself. There is no hard and fast requirement to become an Akurian; we're *too close to god* for most people and a whole lot *too far out* for those of holier-than-thou pretense. We're *Knowers*, not 'believers' as required by The Most High and clearly stated in His Holy Law. And we're perpetually called 'cultists' by all hallelujah halfwits and 'Jesus' praisers in spite of the fact every 'cult' on the planet is a group of 'Jesus' praisers!

346. That, for the time being **(2011 GCAD-5771 Hebrew)** we still have The Living Anointed El Aku ALIHA ASUR HIGH alive among us – to which The Most High, Himself, Testifies – is not only a Singular Honor, but a source of instruction beyond any comparison anywhere else on Earth. His history is contained in **"The ANOINTED, The ELECT, and The DAMNED!"** from his twenty-third year **(1959 GCAD – 5719 Hebrew)** with many references to his experience, earned Rank and Station.

347. To become and remain a True and Righteous Akurian with The Holy Mark of a Proven Knower in your forehead – preempting the Mark of the Beast **(Revelation 13:16-17, 14:9-11, 15:2, 16:2, 19:20 and**

20:4) – really isn't that hard to do. The positions are open to everybody regardless of Race, Mixed Race, sex, age or current lifestyle. Repentance and full **(as possible)** adherence to Holy Law as given in the First Five books of the Old Testament – the Torah, *and not the Talmud* – are absolutes; which does *not* include murdering errant children, or anyone else just because they refuse our invitation or hold some other 'belief.'

348. The Akurians are The Most High's living witnesses and on-scene Judges that when all the Instigators, Manipulators, Marxists, Communists, Fascists, Socialists, Progressives, Politicians, Judges, Journalists, Priests, Preachers and other liars are called before The Most High in Final Judgment and begin their whine: "Lord, you don't know what I was up against; you don't understand the situation;" we step forth and declare, **"I was there!** *Why don't you explain it to me?"*

349. The be a True and Righteous Proven Knower of The Great Testimony is the infinite and absolute Rank and Station all Creation has to offer. To be counted among the True and Righteous, to stand in the Company of the Righteous, and to be called a "Good and Faithful Servant" by The Most High, Himself, is beyond any Earthly Reward.

350. And *that* Rank and Station is open to all who will learn to *know* and not 'believe.'

The Akurians.

www.ingramcontent.com/pod-product-compliance
Lightning Source LLC
Chambersburg PA
CBHW041625220426
43663CB00001B/10